Itei
bel
tel
Fi'
tic
a.
ir
b'

HEROES & VILLAINS
Forgotten Irish Stories

by

Siobhán Mulcahy

CHOMSKY PUBLISHING

First Published in Ireland in 2004
by CHOMSKY PUBLISHING

Cover design by Patrick Brocklebank

British Library Cataloguing in Publication Data
A catalogue record for this book is available from the British Library.

ISBN 0-9546896-0-7

Dedication

To the forgotten Heroes & Villains of Ireland who
have been an inspiration in the writing of this book.

Acknowledgements

I wish to acknowledge the following for their
assistance and co-operation:
Dun Laoghaire Public Library
Dun Laoghaire College of Further Education
The National Archives
The National Library
Dublin City Library & Archive

Special thanks to Brian Smith, Dun Laoghaire and
to Patrick Brocklebank, who designed the cover.

Contents

Preface

There are several common threads running throughout this book. All of the profiles are of Irish people with the exception of Ché Guevara Lynch, who was of Irish descent. His *flamboyance and mad streak* - he shot deserters 'at will'and fell out with almost everyone he ever met - were comparable to those of Lola Montez, the Irish courtesan and dancer from Limerick, who carried a horse whip with her wherever she went and used it on kings as well as paupers. She developed a *drink problem* in later life, as did Captain John Riley, who choked on his own vomit, and Lady Mary Heath, who died from a drink related accident.

Emigration is also a feature in this book. If it were not for the poverty in Ireland during the 19th century alongside the Great Irish Famine, Ché Guevara Lynch's grandmother may not have emigrated from Galway, nor perhaps would Captain John Riley have felt the need to emigrate to America to become a soldier.; Francis Tumblety, who became Jack the Ripper, may not have left his impoverished family in Limerick to live a nefarious existence.

There are several *high achievers* in this book – the two most notable are Lena Rice, who remains Ireland's only female Wimbledon Singles Champion and Lady Mary Heath, who broke world records in athletics and aviation.

Lena Rice's *modesty* can be compared with that of Agnes Clerke from Skibbereen; a brilliant astrophysicist and author of many books who had a crater on the moon named after her. Both these women disappeared into oblivion after their successful careers had ended.

The *militaristic tendencies* of Ché Guevara whose father said he had 'Irish rebel blood in his veins', and Captain John Riley led both men into the pages of revolutionary history. Today, these men are either admired as heroes or despised as traitors in different parts of the globe.

Paganism and the black arts are also covered in the story of Kilkenny woman, Alice Kyteler, otherwise known as the Mother of All Irish Witches. The Catholic Church, the Inquisition; British rule in Ireland under Cromwell, rebellion and war, poverty and slavery, emigration and new horizons, drunkenness and high achievement are all here for your enjoyment.

'Doctor' Francis Tumblety
1833-1903
Jack the Ripper

'Doctor'Francis Tumblety, from
Limerick, circa 1887

In 1888, five women were brutally murdered and disemboweled in the slums of Whitechapel in London. Though there have been many suspects over the years, the chief among them remains an Irishman.

At the time of the murders, Francis Tumblety, a wealthy 'quack' doctor from Limerick boasted of keeping women's organs in pickle jars; he also fitted the description of the killer from eyewitness accounts.

Ripperologists have voted him 'the man most likely to have committed the murders'. But Tumblety died peacefully in his bed just over one hundred years ago. Did Scotland Yard detectives deliberately let him escape?

In Victorian England, the East End of London was set apart from the rest of the city, both economically and socially. Some 900,000 people lived in this teaming slum. Cattle and sheep were herded through the streets of Whitechapel to the slaughterhouses nearby where they were bludgeoned to death.

The screams of the animals could be heard on the streets during the slaughter. The streets themselves were stained with blood and excrement. Rubbish and liquid sewage gave the area a horrible smell. For the most part, the people who lived in the East End were the working poor, the unemployed, the insane and criminals.

The inhabitants of the area lived in tenement houses under deplorable conditions. Almost every single room housed an entire family. Prostitution was one of the only reliable means through which a single woman or widow could maintain herself. The police estimated that in 1888, there were some 1,200 prostitutes in the Whitechapel district, not including the women who supplemented their menial jobs by occasional prostitution.

There were also over 200 common lodging houses in Whitechapel, serving almost 9,000 people. The sleeping rooms contained long rows of beds, often infested with vermin and insects. If a woman had not earned enough money to pay for a bed for the night, she would have to find someone who would let her sleep with him in return for sexual favours. Otherwise she slept on the street.

* * *

The Jack the Ripper murders began on the 31st of August, 1888. The name 'Jack the Ripper' originates from two letters written by someone claiming to be the killer which were published in the newspapers at the time of the murders. The Ripper was not the first serial killer, but he was probably the first to appear in a large city at a time when people had become more literate and the press had become a force for social change.

Every day, the activities of the Ripper were chronicled in the

A cartoon of Jack the Ripper which appeared in the daily papers in 1888. Artists and cartoonists were in big demand to produce sketches of the killer.

newspapers, as were the results of inquiries and actions taken by the police. It was the press coverage that made the series of gruesome murders a "phenomenon" - something the world had never seen before. The killings took place within a square mile area in the districts of Whitechapel, Spitalfields, and Aldgate.

All five victims had worked as occasional prostitutes. Autopsies revealed that the murderer seized the women by their throats and strangled them until they were unconscious or dead, then he set to work with a surgical knife. Stomach fluids from the bodies showed that each woman had been drunk, and very vulnerable, at the time of death.

Polly Nichols, the first victim, was murdered on Friday August 31, 1888. Her body had severe abdominal bruising. Annie Chapman, murdered on Saturday, September 8, 1888, had her uterus and bladder removed. Elizabeth Stride, murdered on Sunday, September 30, 1888, had several body organs, including her bowels, removed. Catherine Eddowes, murdered on the same date, had her left kidney removed.

Mary Kelly, the final victim, was murdered on Friday, November 9, 1888. Her body was mutilated beyond recognition and she had to be identified from what remained of her clothing. When police surgeons attempted to reconstruct her body in the mortuary, they found that her heart had been removed.

There is no evidence to suggest that any of the murdered prostitutes knew each other, unlike the fictional portrayal of the women in the recent film, *From Hell*, starring Johnny Depp as the Chief Detective investigating the case. (In the film, Mary Kelly escapes the Ripper and returns to live happily in Ireland.).

Scotland Yard joined the London City Police in the hunt for the killer and the two forces were co-ordinated by Chief Inspector George Abberlaine.

As the police were under tremendous pressure to solve the murders, they put forward three initial theories:

1. A gang of thieves was responsible,
2. A gang extorting money from prostitutes was killing them for failing to pay protection money,
3. A maniac was on the loose.

At the time, the *London Observer* pointed out sarcastically that "as all the murdered women were the poorest of the poor, the first two options were impossible."

Extra police were put on patrol. Bloodhounds were trained and deployed in the area but it was impossible, even for highly trained dogs, to sniff out the killer in an area reeking from both the slaughterhouses and the flowing excrement on the streets.

Several weeks passed before any eyewitnesses came forward to help the police. The sexual butcher operated at night as the streets of Whitechapel were poorly lit by gas lamps. Though Polly Nichols had been found shortly after her death in Buck's Row, no vehicle or person was seen leaving the scene of the crime.

It was not until Annie Chapman's death in Spitalfields, that a useful eyewitness came forward. A Mrs Elizabeth Long told police that she had seen a "gentleman" talking to Annie shortly before the time of her death. He was a man over forty years of age with whiskers.

"He looked what I should call shabby genteel, and a foreigner to London," she told police.

The double murder of Elizabeth Stride and Kate Eddowes on the night of September 30th brought forward two more witnesses. The first saw Elizabeth Stride talking to a man in a long dark coat, and a peaked cap shortly before the time of her murder. The second witness had left the Imperial Club at 1.35 am, and had seen a man in a deerstalker hat and a dark coat talking with Kate Eddowes nine minutes before the estimated time of her death. The police could now start to build a profile of the killer.

From the testimony of these witnesses, and the results of medical autopsies, the police now had a number of probabilities:

• Jack the Ripper was a white male
• Of average or below average height
• May have been a foreigner to London
• Was between 30-45 years of age in 1888
• Wore a moustache or whiskers
• Wore a long dark coat and a button-down, deer-stalker hat
• Was 'shabby-genteel' in appearance
• Had lodgings in the East End
• Had medical expertise though may not have been well-educated
• Was Right-handed
• Was most likely single (so he was free to roam the streets at night)
• May have been impotent

Insanity and medical qualifications became the key factors in sorting out suspects. Alibis for potential suspects often consisted of confinement in asylums or jails. If someone could prove that he had been confined during one of the murders, then he was dropped from the list. The focus on medical knowledge led police well beyond the reaches of Whitechapel into the middle and upper classes of London, and the eccentric and violent behaviour of some surgeons and doctors was called into question. Several 'foreign' doctors were thrown into lunatic asylums.

The police were under pressure to find the culprit, but when one killing followed another, it was obvious that they were no nearer to solving the mystery. In a time before forensic science or fingerprinting, the only way the police could prove someone committed a murder was to catch the person in the act, find a credible witness or get a suspect to confess.

Tumblety began to fit the profile of Jack the Ripper. He boasted to prostitutes that he kept women's wombs in pickle jars

By the time Mary Kelly was slaughtered, the finger of suspicion began to point firmly at Francis Tumblety, an Irish misogynist and 'medical physician' who was known for harassing Whitechapel's prostitutes and who had boasted of keeping women's organs in pickle jars. When the police received a kidney (probably belonging to victim Catherine Eddowes) which had been preserved in vinegar, Tumblety was arrested on suspicion of the murders.

* * *

First reports of Francis Tumblety are far from promising. In 1848, he was described by his neighbors in Limerick, as 'a dirty, awkward, ignorant, good-for-nothing boy…utterly devoid of education and uncared-for by his family.'

He was born in Ireland in 1833. The name Tumblety has several Irish variations such as Tumelty, Tumulty and O'Tomalty. It originates from the northwest of Ireland, though researchers believe the Tumblety family lived in Limerick where Francis was born into a large, poverty-stricken family.

In 1850, at the tender age of 17, Francis took the boat to America to escape his brutish father and the gloom of post-Famine Ireland. He settled in Detroit where he set himself up as a 'medical physician'. At that time, America was swarming with medical 'quacks' who made money from the sick and the dying.

There is no indication that Tumblety ever finished school or even attended medical training, but despite this important detail, he managed to become quite a prosperous 'doctor' by selling home-made potions and miracle cures to the rich and the vulnerable. He moved across North America, living a flamboyant lifestyle from the proceeds of his trade. Frequently, he fell foul of the law and would quickly move location to set up his 'practice' in another area – always one step ahead of the police. In 1865, he was arrested near Washington as a suspect in President Lincoln's assassination, but it turned out to be a case of mistaken identity.

*Chief Inspector John George
Littlechild: "One of the main suspects is a
quack called Tumblety who was a frequent
visitor to Whitechapel at the time of the
killings. On these occasions, he was
constantly brought under the notice of police
and there is a large dossier concerning him
at Scotland Yard."*

Francis Tumblety was known for despising women, especially 'fallen women'. According to the *Baltimore City Paper*, he collected "women's uteri [wombs] in medical jars" and called all women "cattle". When he moved to New York in the early 1880s, he came to the attention of the police because of his 'mania for the company of young men and grown-up youths'. At that time, any homosexual act was a criminal offence.

In order to avoid the police, Tumblety moved to London in June 1888, shortly before the Whitechapel murders began. The eccentric 'pills and potions man' was arrested within a fortnight for 'acts of gross indecency' (which was Victorian-speak for homosexual activity) in the Whitechapel district. As the courts and prisons in East London were swamped with criminals at the time, Tumblety was fined for his 'sins' and immediately released.

While the murders were taking place, he came to police attention again because he began to fit the profile of the killer. He was known in the district for threatening prostitutes on the streets - though this was a fairly common practice among men in the district.

He boasted of keeping women's organs, particularly their wombs, in preserves of vinegar. He wore military style clothing, with long dark coats, and often wore a button-down, deer stalker hat similar to the one eyewitnesses said the killer had worn. He insisted that everyone called him 'Doctor', and though he was a 'quack', he may have had enough knowledge of anatomy to perform the gruesome disembowelments.

At the time of the murders, hundreds of letters (mostly hoaxes) were sent to the police and news agencies associated with solving the case. Only three letters stood out as having any significance whatsoever. The two letters signed 'Jack the Ripper' were eventually discounted because the red stains on the paper were found to be red ink rather than blood stains.

George Lusk, the head of the Mile End Vigilance Committee in Whitechapel, received the only other letter of significance - most probably written by the real killer. This time, the letter was sent with a parcel containing a portion of a human kidney.

Post-marked 16th October 1888, it was full of spelling mistakes, had no punctuation at all, and had the phonetic spelling of someone with an Irish accent or background. (Notice the words "Sor" and "Mishter" below).

From Hell
Mr Lusk
Sor
I send you half the Kidne I took one women prasarved it for you tother piece I fried and ate it was very nise I may send you the bloody knif that took it out if you only wate a whil longer
Signed
Catch me when you can
Mishter Lusk

The letter was copied and posted outside every police station in the hope that someone would recognise the handwriting. A facsimile of the letter was published in all the London daily papers.

The portion of kidney accompanying the letter was examined by Dr Thomas Openshaw at the London Hospital. It was found to be a human adult kidney, which had been preserved in spirits of vinegar rather than the formalin fluid used in hospitals.

Dr Openshaw also indicated that the kidney belonged to a person suffering from Bright's Disease, the same disease which had afflicted the Ripper's fourth victim, Kate Eddowes.

By the time these new facts came to light, Mary Kelly had already been butchered to death on November 9th 1888. Queen Victoria was furious about the murder of Mary Kelly. "This new most ghastly murder shows the absolute necessity for some very decided action. All these streets must be properly lit, and our detectives improved. They are not what they should be" she told her Prime Minister.

Several prostitutes came forward claiming Tumblety was the culprit because he had gloated publicly about wanting to take his knife to them, and because his appearance also matched previous eyewitness accounts published in the media.

The Irish girl with the long red hair and the slender limbs, had been the most savagely disfigured of all the Whitechapel victims. Criminologists believe that Tumblety, who never shrank from declaring his hatred of women - especially prostitutes – must certainly have hated the memory of his brutal childhood in Ireland.

Mary Kelly, likeTumblety, had originated from Co. Limerick. Ripperologists now claim that this 'double trigger' probably led to the increased ferocity of the attack.

When questioned by police, Tumblety could not account for his whereabouts at the times of the brutal slayings and he was charged on suspicion of the Whitechapel murders shortly after (what was left of) Mary Kelly's body was found in her lodgings.

Incredibly, after his arrest and a single court appearance, the Limerick-man was released on bail on 24th November 1888. There is some suspicion that because he had become wealthy from his 'medical practices', he could easily have bribed the court judge in order to secure his release.

He immediately fled to France, from where he was able to return to America. Police in New York were waiting for him, and he was charged with 'acts of gross indecency' for homosexual acts. He was never charged for the Ripper murders 'because there was not sufficient proof that he was implicated.' Eyewitness accounts in London suggested that Jack the Ripper was aged between 30-45 years. By the year 1888, Francis Tumblety was already in his 50s.

Scotland Yard detectives pursued him to America, but the Irishman was a master of evasion and quickly moved from New York to another city. He continued to peddle his drugs and potions to the rich and the vulnerable, but now he operated on a mail-order only basis.

20

*Queen Victoria's grandson, Prince Albert, Victor,
Duke of Clarence – better known as 'Eddy" -
became a popular suspect in the 1960s. Eddy
was as far away as Scotland at the time of some
of the killings.*

In summing up the case, Chief Inspector John Littlechild wrote in his police notes: "One of the main suspects is a quack called Tumblety who was a frequent visitor to Whitechapel at the time of the killings. On these occasions, he was constantly brought under the notice of police and there is a large dossier concerning him at Scotland Yard."

"Although he was deemed to be a 'Sycopathia Sexualis' he was not known as a sadist, which the murderer unquestionably was, but his feelings of hatred towards women were remarkable and bitter in the extreme, a fact on record".

In Tumblety's defence, Littlechild concluded that a few factors appeared to disqualify him as a credible suspect:

"He was 55 years old at the time of the killings, a bit too old, according to some eye witness accounts. Also, homosexual serial killers usually prey upon their own sex, not the opposite sex," he concluded.

The London Metropolitan Police officially closed the Jack the Ripper case, marking it as 'Unsolved' in 1892.

Francis Tumblety continued to fear capture for the rest of his life and he never stayed very long in any one place. In 1900, the US census shows that he was living at 218-220 Liberty Street, Baltimore. Death records show that he died in St Louis in 1903.

After the Irishman's hasty exit from London, other misfits and maniacs were suspected of the killings but there was never enough evidence to pin the killings on any of them. In the vacuum that existed, both the media and fiction writers began to take on the role of investigator and the legend of the Ripper continued.

Plots involving Freemasons, royal physicians and sinister occult figures were paraded before the public as the final solution to the Ripper case. Queen Victoria's grandson, Prince Albert, Victor, Duke of Clarence – better known as 'Eddy" - became a popular suspect in the 1960s. But Eddy was as far away as Scotland at the time of some of the killings. Royal physician, Sir William Gull was also put forward as a candidate, even though he was suffering from paralysis in 1888.

The most recent suspect came to light in late 2001, when Patricia Cornwell, best-selling crime writer suggested in her book, *Portrait of a Killer: Jack the Ripper – Case Closed*, that the impressionist painter William Sickert was the real Jack the Ripper. Cornwell is believed to have spent $4 million of her own money trying to prove her theory, even buying some of Sickert's expensive paintings (and apparently ripping them up) in the hope of finding hidden evidence. Her theory rests on the fact that Sickert painted prostitutes in Whitechapel district during 1888, so he must, in fact, be the real killer. Most Ripperologists believe this theory is nonsense; they voted Francis Tumblety 'the man most likely to have been Jack the Ripper' in 2002.

As much of the original evidence from the case in 1888 has either been lost or stolen by Ripper entusiasts, writers and others, it is unlikely that the Whitechapel murders will ever be solved.

Helena Grace Rice
1866-1907
Forgotten Wimbledon Champion

*A ladylike Lena Rice photographed just
prior to the Wimbledon Final, 1890*

When Lena Rice, from Co. Tipperary walked onto
Wimbledon's Centre Court to compete in the 1890
Ladies Singles Final, the 300-strong audience clapped
politely. They were about to see something that would set
tongues wagging in "polite society" and something that would
change the way women's tennis was played forever.

Though she remains the only Irishwoman to have won the
Wimbledon Championship, today Lena Rice lies buried and
almost completely forgotten in a small Tipperary graveyard.

It is more than one hundred and twenty five years since 200 spectators paid a shilling each to watch Spencer Gore win the first Lawn Tennis Championships at Wimbledon. In those days, it was a Gentlemen's Singles event only, and the champion received a Silver Challenge Cup and the Gold Prize of twelve guineas. Just 22 men had entered the first tournament.

The Ladies Singles competition did not begin until 1884, when Ms Maud Watson triumphed from a group of only 13 entrants. As Ladies champion, she received prize money of a paltry seven guineas.

Today, Wimbledon is watched by millions of people worldwide on satellite television with total prize money of more than 2.5 million Sterling. Meanwhile, in a tiny cemetery in Downey's Field in the village of New Inn, Co. Tipperary, the only Irish woman to win the All England Tennis Championships at Wimbledon lies buried and forgotten.

Lena Rice, who won the coveted title in 1890, aged 24 years, played tennis for only two seasons during a brief, yet very successful, career. Few Irish people know that she ever existed.

The Wimbledon *Biography of Champions* states that "Her distinction in the saga of Wimbledon's heroines is that she qualifies as the least distinguished".

The brief biography (of five lines) makes no mention of the fact that Lena Rice was the first woman to officiate at Wimbledon, or that it was she who introduced the forehand smash into the women's game. Lena Rice's Irishness is also overlooked.

Lena, (who was Christened Helena Bertha Grace) was the second youngest of the seven children of Spring Rice and Anna Gorde. She was born on 21st June 1866 at Marlhill, in a two-storied Georgian building, half a mile from New Inn, Co. Tipperary

She had two brothers, Henry and Spring, and four sisters, Bess, Connie, Annie and Lucy. Her father was a cousin of Mary Spring-Rice, and a friend of Erskine Childers, who took part with him in the Howth gun-running on *The Aud* in 1914.

Lena, who regularly partnered her sister Annie at tennis, learnt the game at home, where her parents entertained in their large garden at Marlhill in the 1880s. The family fortunes were not to last, and after the death of Spring Rice, the household declined into a state of near destitution.

Up to the time of their father's death, the two sisters played regularly at Cahir Lawn Tennis Club, which had four courts as well as two croquet lawns. Lena's tennis skills developed quickly - no doubt helped along by the fact that most of her early opponents were men.

She had a very powerful service game, and a forehand drive that put many of her male counterparts to shame. With a British cavalry regiment stationed near Cahir, mixed tennis became very fashionable in the district at the time.

According to the Wimbledon Museum, "Lawn tennis was played right from the outset by ladies as well as gentlemen. As a garden party pastime, it provided the perfect social opportunity for young men and women to meet over a gentle game of mixed doubles."

It was a game exclusive to the rich (including Britain's royal family) because the lower classes could not afford the expensive racquets, balls and membership of private clubs that were then a requirement of the game.

In those days, tennis was an extremely dangerous sport. The balls were made from leather, stuffed with wool or hair, and were hard enough to cause serious injury and even death. It was not until the late 1870's that India rubber (made from a vulcanisation process invented by Charles Goodyear) was used to manufacture tennis balls especially for tournaments.

Also, the rubber balls were so rare and expensive that players practicing prior to matches (no matter how rich) were obliged to "make do" with leather balls similar to those used in cricket or hockey today.

Due to the propriety of the time, women were expected to cover their arms and legs while playing the game. Boned corsets and layers of petticoats, floor length skirts and high-necked blouses, made it almost impossible for them to bend down to pick up the tennis balls. The solution to this problem was the "tennis apron" which was often beautifully embroidered, and furnished with large pockets to accommodate the heavy balls.

While women were obliged to wear dresses that were tight where they should have been loose, men wore well-cut cream or white flannel trousers with long-sleeved flannel shirts, silk ties, and kerchiefs or sashes around the waist. Both male and female players were obliged to wear straw boater hats as it was the custom of the day.

Dublin, despite the poverty of many of its inhabitants, had a glittering social life at the time. During the "season", debutantes came up to Dublin to be presented to the Viceroy, the King's representative in Ireland. The young ladies stayed in the Shelbourne Hotel in Stephen's Green or in the big Georgian mansions in Fitzwilliam and Merrion Square.

Wimbledon Champions such as Miss Maud Watson, Mrs Blanche Hillyard and the famous "Lottie" Dod had begun to come over to Dublin to "farm" the Irish tournaments, so the competition was very tough and it was rare to have an Irish champion at the Irish tournaments.

Lena Rice's first sporting appearance outside Co. Tipperary was at the Irish Championships at the Fitzwilliam Lawn Tennis Club in May 1889. Her sister Annie, who also played, but usually lost in the first round, continued to travel with her sister as a 'chaperone'. At Fitzwilliam, Lena lost narrowly in two sets to Mrs Hillyard – five times Wimbledon Champion - in the semi-final. She was able to extract some revenge in the Mixed Doubles, when partnered by Willoughby Hamilton, she won the Mixed Doubles title, beating Mrs Hillyard and Henry Stone in the final, 6-4, 5-7, 6-4.

*Lena Rice, ready to receive the ball, during
the Wimbledon Final, 1890*

In June that year, she competed at the Lansdowne Handicap Challenge in Dublin where she was runner up in the Women's Singles tournament. She then crossed to England (with Annie) to compete at Wimbledon for the first time. Though she battled hard to get to the final, Lena found that Mrs Hillyard, who had become something of a nemesis, was again to be her opponent.

After almost two hours on court, the Irishwoman had three match points to become the Wimbledon Champion of 1889. She was winning in the final set: 4-3; 40-30, when she lost her nerve and faltered. Mrs Hillyard managed to recover to win the next three games, taking the title, 4-6, 8-6, 6-4.

Even by today's standards, it was a long and gruelling match, containing a total of 34 games. Lena returned to Ireland "disappointed and exhausted".

Again, the following year, during the 1890 Irish Fitzwilliam Championships, Lena lost the women's singles final, this time, to Louise Martin, 9-7, 6-4 - a match she had been expected to win. The newspapers of the day commented acidly that Ms Rice "had fallen to pieces as usual under pressure".

The *Irish Times*, Saturday, May 31st 1890:

"There was again a great throng of faultlessly costumed ladies with their attendant male escorts in Fitzwilliam Square yesterday when some brilliant play was witnessed under the most favourable circumstances."

"The weathermen forecast wet and dreary weather but were proven wrong and no showers fell which would have spoiled the tournament at its most crucial point and have hidden the brilliantly fashioned spring dresses beneath hideous rain cloaks, and hidden fair faces under widespread and gloomy umbrellas."

"The final match of the Ladies Championship Singles was started on Court 5. Ms Rice started by winning the first set to love, but Ms Martin, who became accustomed to the wind, followed with the second."

"In the final set, it was 4 games each when Ms Martin took the 9th game and Ms Rice took the next two games. The 12th game was a love game to Ms Martin. Ms Rice then went to pieces and Ms Martin won the next game and the match."

Despite the stinging criticism, Lena went on to win both the Women's Doubles and Mixed Doubles titles during the Fitzwilliam tournament. When, several weeks later, she won her first Ladies Singles title, 6-3, 6-1 at the Lansdowne Handicap event, the Irish media quickly changed their tune. They even began to speculate about whether she could win at Wimbledon. They also piled on the pressure:

"Ms Rice has greatly improved since last year and it is doubtful whether she has an equal in the Lawn Tennis world this season. Irish eyes will be watching her expectantly at Wimbledon. Mrs Hillyard is not defending her title this year as she is now pregnant. Ms Rice will never again have a better opportunity to win the tournament."

As expected, Lena had little difficulty reaching the final, where her opponent was to be Miss M. Jacks of Great Britain. She had beaten her easily (6-2, 6-0) in the previous year's semi-final so things were looking good for an Irish victory. It was a brilliantly sunny day on that 4th of July and the crowd were expecting a good match. Lena Rice's opponent in the Wimbledon final was a Miss Jacks - a newcomer to the game of tennis - had battled courageously in all her matches to reach the final.

Both ladies wore full-length dresses with long sleeves, bustles, corsets and long petticoats. On their coiffeured heads, they wore boater hats to protect their delicate faces from the harsh sunlight. This was the acceptable fashion for ladies tennis at the time. According to a newspaper account: "Ms Rice wore a two piece costume, comprising an ankle length floral-patterned skirt and a blouse tightly clinched to the waist." Though men were allowed to leap and dive around the court, women were expected to run in a "ladylike fashion" never exposing their ankles as they ran. In any event, their heavy corsets and petticoats made it almost impossible for them to play the game in an athletic way.

The Irishwoman won the first set 6-4, without much incident, but was frustrated in the second when her opponent started to make a comeback. In what turned out to be the final game of the match, Lena Rice stunned everyone.

"After a promising start, Ms Rice lost her concentration, allowing Miss Jacks to get back into the game. The contest was much closer than anyone expected, though the Irishwoman won the first set, which had been very close, at 6-4. When the games stood at 4-4 in the second set, it looked as though the match would go into a third and final set."

When Miss Jacks hit a looping ball into her opponent's side of the court it, bounced almost to head height. The Irish woman must have decided that enough was enough - she wanted to finish off the match quickly. She leaped into the air and pointing her racket downwards, smashing the ball onto her opponent's side of the court. Having bounced inside her opponent's baseline, the ball skidded high into the air and out beyond the back row of the arena.

The normally sedate Wimbledon crowd gasped with a mixture of awe and admiration, and there was a long pause before loud clapping broke out around the audience. Not only had Lena Rice polished off the match convincingly, she had - in one stroke - introduced the forehand smash into the ever-so-polite world of women's tennis.

The newspaper report described it as follows:

"Then Ms Rice made a final push for victory and polished off the match by taking the last two games of the second set without losing a single point. She won the match by a margin of 6-4, 6-4 by smashing the ball in an unladylike fashion onto her opponent's side of the court."

Lena Rice, from Tipperary, was aged 24 years and 14 days on her day of glory and had scored 58 points to her opponent's 42.

*Charlotte (Lottie) Dod, Great
Britian, became the youngest player
ever to win a Wimbledon singles
event when, in 1887; she won at the
age of 15 years, 285 days. She didn't
have to wear a restrictive corset as
she was too young. She wore her
school uniform instead.*

She was presented with the 50 guineas Challenge Trophy, together with a cash prize of 20 guineas, a gold bracelet and a ring set with diamonds and emeralds. Luck must have been with the Irish during that particular Wimbledon tournament, as the following day, Willoughby Hamilton, from Dublin triumphed in the men's singles tournament.

Lena Rice retired from competitive tennis immediately after her Wimbledon victory. It can only be assumed that due to her mother's deteriorating health, and the family's lack of money, she was prevented from continuing her tennis career. Her mother died in 1891, after struggling for many years to manage the household finances following her husband's death.

Little is known of Lena's life after 1890. It seems she retreated back into ordinary life. After her mother's death, she lived alone at Marlhill where her social world revolved around the local church at New Inn and included various charitable works. In the census of 1901, she is ascribed the title of "landowner".

On 21st June 1907, just 17 years after her Wimbledon triumph, Lena Rice, who never married, died of tuberculosis on her 41st birthday. She was buried close to her parents in the local cemetery. In her last Will & Testament, she left twenty-five pounds to Doctor Bernardo's homes for children and a further twenty-five pounds to the New Inn church for the restoration of its yard wall.

"I bequeath my Wimbledon gold bracelet to my friend Ms Parker and my Fitzwilliam Lawn Tennis clock and my diamond and emerald Wimbledon ring to my friends, Claud and Nellie Johnston" she wrote in her own hand.

By that stage, hats and bustles had disappeared from women's tennis, although long skirts and petticoats were still the norm. It was therefore quite shocking when the legendary French player, Suzanne Lenglen, appeared at Wimbledon in 1919 in a flimsy cotton dress without petticoats or a corset. It was even more sensational when an American woman, nicknamed "Gorgeous Gussie" Moran,

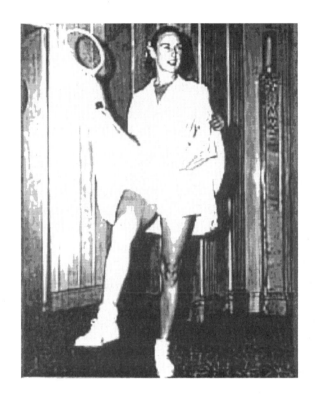

'Gorgeous' Gussie Moran pictured in 1949. Her knickers appeared on the front pages of newspapers and magazines across the world. Though she never progressed beyond the second round of any major tournament, a racehorse, an aircraft, and a special cooking sauce were named after her.

wore lace-trimmed panties and a short skirt at the Championships in 1949. Gussie and her knickers appeared on the front pages of newspapers and magazines across the world. And though she never progressed beyond the second round in any major tournament, a racehorse, an aircraft, and a special cooking sauce were named after her.

In the three decades that followed Gussie's brief appearance on the world stage, frilly knickers became *de rigeur* for women tennis players at all major tournaments. But by 1979, the habit of wearing the silly tennis undergarment had lost its appeal, and Virginia Wade was the last woman to wear the apparel in a tennis final. By that stage, women players wanted to wear whatever they liked so long as this followed the general rule of being 'predominantly white'. A decade would pass before Martina Navratilova became the first woman to wear shorts in a Wimbledon final.

In 1990, on the 100th anniversary of the Lena Rice's victory, Navratilova became the only woman to win the women's singles title for a record nine times. Throughout her career, she had used the forearm smash, invented by the Irishwoman, to perfection.

* * *

Wimbledon Champions, Rice and Hamilton were not the only Irish players to grace the famous grass arena. An Irishman called Vere (St Leger) Goold became so demoralised by his defeat in the Wimbledon Men's singles final in 1879 that he fell into an abyss from which he never recovered. He later committed murder and died in prison.

The son of the resident Waterford magistrate, Goold worked as a secretary at the Municipal Boundaries Commission in Dublin - a job that gave him plenty of time to play tennis. He was described as an athletic young man with the world at his feet.

According to Fitzwilliam Tennis Club's *History of Irish Tennis*, he was the bright spark of the tennis club during these years. In the minutes of tennis committee meetings, his name is constantly mentioned. "Mr Goold was selected to handicap". "Mr Goold reported that he had ordered four nets from Messrs. Caylers at £1 each and they had promised to present one net to the club."

He won the men's singles title at Fitzwilliam in 1879, beating a Mr Barry in the final, 8-6, 8-6 to become Ireland's national champion. Apparently, he had a 'splendid backhand' and was confidently expected to win the All England title at Wimbledon later the same year. Unfortunately, his plans were scuppered when the Rev JT Hartley beat him in the final.

Twenty years later, Goold found himself in a Monte Carlo courtroom accused of murdering and then dismembering a woman's body. He and his wife, a French woman, had robbed and stabbed a Swedish lady and sent her dismembered remains back to England in a trunk. The crime was only discovered when the Swedish woman's blood was seen oozing from the trunk as it went through customs in England. When Goold was traced with his wife to Marseilles, he was arrested carrying the dead woman's head in a hatbox.

At his trial, the Irishman tried to take all the blame for the heinous act while his wife only admitted to "helping her husband to dismember the body".

The French court found the opposite to be the case - it was she who had committed the murder and Goold had merely helped her to dispose of the body. She was condemned to death while the former tennis ace, who had become a hopeless alcoholic by this stage, received a life sentence without reprieve.

He was sent to Devil's Island prison where he died in 1908.

Countess Lola Montez
1818-1861
Irish Courtesan who ruled Bavaria

*Lola Montez (neé Dolores Gilbert)
painted in 1847 by Joseph Stieler*

When a man met Lola Montez, her reputation automatically made him think of bedrooms. It was said that her beauty, particularly the splendour of her breasts, made madmen everywhere.

For 18 months during 1847-8, Limerick born Lola became the lover of King Ludwig I of Bavaria. Her control over the king was so intense that she became the *de facto* ruler of the German province. The dancer and courtesan's wild behaviour was extremely exciting and she was a gift to the gutter press. Readers from every class could take sides over the issue of the king's lover.

During her heyday, the Irishwoman was so notorious that tradesmen in Germany became prosperous by selling trinkets and cigarette boxes bearing her image.

Dolores ('Lola') Eliza Gilbert was born in Limerick, Ireland in 1818. Her father was an officer in the King's Scottish regiment who had earned his commission for courage during the Napoleonic Wars. Her mother was the beautiful Eliza Oliver, who, according to Lola's' memoirs, descended from an impoverished Spanish grandee who had brought his family to Ireland during the reign of Ferdinand and Isabella. Lola's mother was not in fact Spanish; she was the illegitimate daughter of Charles Oliver, who was at one time a member of the Irish parliament.

Lola often lied about her origins. Sometimes she was the illegitimate daughter of Lord Byron, and sometimes, depending on her mood, the daughter of a Spanish matador. This cherished but erroneous story prompted Lola's choice of a professional theatrical name of 'Montez' when she later became a dancer.

Her parents left Ireland to live in 'the India of the British Raj' in 1923 where her father rejoined his regiment in Dinapore. The little girl, known as 'Lola', the diminutive of her first name, Dolores, became the darling of the regiment. Her dark black curls and stunning blue eyes could capture the hearts of men even when she was a child. Everyone she met spoilt her because of her beauty.

Lola was heartbroken when her father died of cholera within a year and her mother married his best friend, a Lieutenant Craigie. She was shipped 'home' to get an education; first to Dublin and then to Scotland, where her strict Presbyterian relatives were unable to 'tame' her violent temper. They sent her to (even more distant relatives) in London. Finally, she was sent to an expensive finishing school in Paris where she developed a gift for languages. She also developed her anti-clerical prejudices and an interest in politics.

Lola and her mother had the same volatile character, and in the ten years they were apart, neither had missed the other. Mrs Craigie, who had received regular reports of her wild and stubborn daughter, decided when Lola returned to India that it was time for her to marry. She wanted a 'return on her financial investment' and arranged a wedding for her daughter with a wealthy, sixty-year-old judge.

In despair, the 18-year-old Lola married the first man she could find, which turned out to be a young British officer called Thomas James. They eloped to Dublin where they spent the next six months regretting their hasty marriage – each being unfaithful to the other whenever the opportunity presented itself. When they eventually returned to India, Thomas James left her to pursue a series of other women. Though Lola wanted a divorce, which was social suicide for a woman at the time, she could never determine exactly where to send the papers and she eventually forgot about her marriage altogether. She set off for Europe to pursue a career in the Performing Arts, whereupon her mother renounced her completely and refused to give her any financial help. Her stepfather however, who had always admired her physical charms, was persuaded to give her a cheque for £1,000.

Arriving first in Spain, Lola began to absorb the culture and the language. She wanted to become an actress, but immediately learned that she couldn't act. She acquired the basic moves of Flamenco dancing and changed her name to Lola 'Montez' to give herself an authentic sounding 'Spanish' monogram. In 1843, she appeared in London as 'Lola Montez, the Spanish Dancer' but her first performance was apparently dreadful, as she couldn't dance either. The show closed to hisses, boos, and catcalls. In Lola's view, the oafs in the audience were too ignorant to recognise that a star had been born.

In an attempt to resurrect her flagging career, she invented her 'Tarantula Dance', for which she would later become infamous. In it, she wore flesh-colored body tights with layers of chiffon circling her waist and several 'tarantula sized' cork spiders dangling from the cloth. Lola would spin and twirl in jerking movements to flick the furry spiders off her skirt, writhing more frantically as the dance went on.

One newspaper reported: "While she was dancing, she held the attention of all; their eyes followed the sinuous swaying of her body, now indicating glowing passion, now a light playfulness. Not until she ceased her rhythmic movements was the spell broken. The audience went mad with rapture, and the entire dance had to be repeated over and over again."

Most of the other reviews of her 'spider dance' were scathing and the boo-ing and catcalls continued at each performance. Lola left London for central Europe, where she hoped to receive a better reception. For several years, she took irregular dancing engagements wherever she found them, and her string of lovers and admirers grew. So did her temper.

When a man annoyed her, she would slash him across the face with the whip she always carried. On one occasion, when a lover disappointed her, she fired her pistol at the luckless Romeo as he dodged the ricocheting bullets while escaping down the street with his pants around his knees.

When she wanted to impress, Lola Montez was charming, very charming. In Warsaw, she gave a command performance for the Viceroy of Poland, who was immediately besotted by her and asked her to become his mistress. He offered her his best country estate and mounds of diamonds if she agreed. While appreciating that someone had finally seen her as the *artiste* she was, Lola found his toadlike appearance so repulsive that she refused. The enraged Viceroy decided to destroy her artistic reputation and had stooges placed at her next performance to boo her throughout her dance.

When the Irishwoman learned who was behind the changing attitudes of her audience, she stopped the show and explained to the crowd exactly what was happening. The audience began to riot and the mob spilled out into the streets, to the great chagrin and embarrassment of the Viceroy (not to mention his wife and other mistress.)

A portrait of Ludwig by Joseph Stieler - painted when he was in his thirties. By the time Lola Montez met him, he was already in his sixties. He immediately fell in love with the Irish courtesan.

Fearing retribution, Lola sought asylum in the French embassy, where the ambassador helped to smuggle her out of the country. During a brief tour of St. Petersburg, Lola had a 'private audience' with Tsar Nicholas I, receiving 1,000 roubles for services provided. Proceeding on to a tour of Paris, she found that mid 19th Parisians were not ready for such an avant-garde artist as herself. She was booed once again, and this time she lost her temper, removing her garters and throwing them at the audience in a rage. Seeing that she was hot blooded, audiences began to boo her on purpose, solely to watch her remove her garters. Things were not moving in the direction Lola wanted, and she began carrying her whip onstage to tame the rowdier elements of the front rows.

In Dresden, she met the composer Franz Liszt, and the two enjoyed a burning passion, until Lola became jealous of the attention Liszt received from his legion of admirers. On one occasion, just to upstage him, she burst in on a banquet dedicating a statue to Beethoven, leaping up on the table to dance among the dishes, spilling consommé into the lap of a Duke. After several weeks, Liszt (who had a reputation as the greatest lover of the age) was so completely worn out by Lola, that as she slept, he locked her into their hotel room and fled the district. At the front desk he left a generous sum of money for the furniture he knew she would smash when she awoke.

It was in Paris that she met the great love of her life, Henry Dujarier. A very wealthy, cultured man, who introduced Lola to the leading figures of the day, including Chopin and George Sand, Alexandre Dumas, Victor Hugo and Balzac. Lola and Dujarier enjoyed the cultural and intellectual life in Paris, discussing politics, religion and philosophy. At last, it seemed Lola had met someone who could hold her interest - someone who was able to keep her volatile temper in check. Their happiness did not last however, and the unlucky man was killed in a duel defending the Irishwoman's honour in 1846. It was said afterwards, that someone had interfered with the firing mechanism in Dujarier's pistol and therefore his death had been murder. A six month investigation was launched but nothing conclusive was ever proven.

A disconsolate Lola Montez arrived in Bavaria in September 1847 and installed herself in Munich's best hotel, the Goldener Hirsch. Her reputation had preceded her and she was engaged by the State Theatre to do several performances of her spider dance. But when she arrived for her first rehearsal, the theatre manager took one look at her performance and fired her on the spot, claiming her work was appallingly bad.

Infuriated by this reception, Lola rushed to the nearby palace to appeal her case directly to the King. Still in costume, she charged right into King Ludwig's private study, demanding 'justice'. According to one account, she snatched a pair of scissors from his desk and slit the front of her dress to the waist, revealing nature's perfection. According to another, she used the dagger she always carried to rip the front of her bodice. Seeing how distracted the king was by the tear in her garment, Lola ripped the bodice off completely, so that she could have his undivided attention. She immediately secured a substantial engagement at the Munich Theatre. The manager was fired without notice.

Shortly after their first meeting, Ludwig commissioned Josef Stieler to paint a portrait of the Irishwoman for his Gallery of Beauties. During the sittings, dancer and patron conversed in Spanish on every possible subject. Overcome by both her wild Irish beauty and intelligence (Lola spoke four languages), Ludwig fell hopelessly in love with her. He gave her a substantial allowance directly from the public treasury. He built her a splendid little palace, and he himself designed a marble fountain for the garden which sprayed perfumed water in its plume. He also gave her a gold trimmed coach, upholstered in ermine, the official fur of Royalty.

In the eyes of this ruler who had spent his life in pursuit of beauty and filled his capital with the fruits of his life's quest, the ravishing

Lola appeared before him as the greatest work of art in his kingdom. Within a month of their first meeting, Ludwig had added a codicil to his Will, bequeathing 100,000 gulden to Lola on condition that she was neither married nor widowed at the time of his death. He also gave her an income of 2,400 gulden per year payable by his heir. Ludwig was already in his late 60's when they met, and Lola easily began to rule his imagination and his kingdom. The Bavarian government could not act without the king's say-so, and as the king visited his mistress every day for advice, she became the *de facto* ruler of the Province.

Ludwig's bouquets to Lola were poems:
"By thee my life becomes ennobled,
which without thee was alone and empty,
Thy love is the food of my heart,
without it, I will surely die".

But his Irish courtesan was more interested in politics than in the king's romantic love. She wrote in her diary, shortly after they met: "I exposed the king to the duplicity and villainy of his Prime Minister, Baron Abel, a Jesuit, who has wormed his way into the king's confidence."

Queen Thérèse did not object to Lola's regular presence at the palace and was said to address her as 'my dear' when they spoke together. Her box at the theatre was adjacent to the royal couple's and when she appeared to watch a show, she caused a stir in the audience. Her small frame, flashing blue eyes and black hair made her beauty even more obvious, especially when she wore the exquisite gowns and jewels the king had given her.

'Whatever Lola wants, Lola gets!' was the cry in the streets of Munich as treasures from the city's museums were removed to furnish Lola's little palace. While shopping in Munich, Lola would exclaim when handed the bill: 'You know me, my Ludwig will pay!'

Yet, as with all courtesans, she remained insecure. Whenever

A brooch made with the image of Lola Montez. Businessmen in Munich made money out of trinkets bearing her image while she was King Ludwig's mistress

the king left her for a few days, as he did in the summer of 1847, (Lola was frantic with worry that he might fall under another's influence), she bombarded him with letters and joined him as soon as she could.

Lola kept an English bulldog as a pet. When walking the streets with the animal, she carried a large whip to control him. She often failed to do so and the dog bit tradesmen and passers-by with equal abandon. It was also rumoured that the dog had a particular dislike for Jesuits. Everything she did was reported in the newspapers. Anonymous letters arrived at the palace accusing her of immoral acts, of taking her bodyguards as lovers, of undressing in front of her open window, and of forcing her dressmakers to fit her clothes to her naked body. But efforts to separate Ludwig from 'the dancer' failed to have the desired effect.

When Pope Pious IX wrote to Ludwig complaining that he had 'strayed from the path of virtue', the king's anger against the Jesuits grew. In response, he promised Lola, who had no papers, Bavarian citizenship for her loyalty to the crown. When Prime Minister Von Abel heard about the plan, he was violently opposed to the idea. He and his ministers threatened to resign from the cabinet.

"National feeling is deeply wounded because Bavaria considers she is being ruled by a foreigner, who, on account of her reputation, is condemned by public opinion".

Ludwig accepted his government's resignation and Lola's enemies despaired when he appointed new ministers who were known to be anti-clerical and more liberal about 'moral matters.'

When a popular Catholic professor publicly criticised the king for his actions, Ludwig obliged him to resign. Soon afterwards, a demonstration by Catholic students in favour of the professor developed into a riot outside Lola's house. She reacted by throwing them sweets from her balcony.

When the newspapers asked her who she saw most often, she replied sarcastically: "The rabble and the king".

In an act of retribution for the student revolt, Ludwig had the remaining Catholic professors removed from the University. "I will never abandon Lola," the King said, "My crown for Lola!"

The liberals in Bavarian society were delighted, and for a time, Lola's popularity soared. She was the person who had freed the people from ten years of oppressive clerical domination, and even the media grudgingly praised her in the newspapers as 'an able politician'.

The archconservative Austrian Prince Metternich, who ruled Europe between the two Napoleons sensed disaster and offered Lola the equivalent of $250,000 if she would go away quietly. She threw the money back in his emissary's face.

Shopkeepers were doing excellent business in trinkets, tie-pins, cigarette cases and tobacco boxes bearing her portrait. Encouraged by the surge in the popularity of his mistress, Ludwig decided to fulfill his promise to her by granting her Bavarian citizenship with the title of Countess of Landsfeld. She now owned a large estate with a royal salary of 20,000 florins annually.

Not everyone was happy with the changes in Bavaria's government. The leader of the Opposition, Count Arco-Valee offered 5,000 gulden to the people of Munich 'on the day Lola Montez is deposed'. Students from Munich University held protest marches against 'the dancer's interference in government'. They went to her house and threw rocks at her windows and shouted all kinds of abuse at her. Lola responded by opening her balcony windows and toasting them with a glass of champagne.

When the king heard of the latest demonstrations against his lover, he was outraged, and on 8 February 1848, he closed Munich University completely. The order had dire consequences and there were more riots in the main streets. Two thousand Burghers signed a petition urging Ludwig to change his mind about closing the university. - the students brought much needed business to the city. Ludwig ignored their petition.

Lola was now drunk on power. She had never learnt self-control and her rages and tantrums in public increased. Though she was arrested for striking a waiter with her whip because his service was 'too slow', she was immediately released on Ludwig's orders. In desperation, the king sent her to a witch doctor 'to drive out the evil spirits' but nothing changed.

As the stories about the Irishwoman in the media became more pernicious, ladies in polite society drew aside their children and their skirts as she passed. Rooms would empty whenever she entered. A royal courtesan who flaunted her role and trod the boards could not be allowed access to society's drawing rooms. The royal favourite had become the perfect scapegoat. *The Times* in London suggested that the Irishwoman who claimed to be Spanish would be 'the cause of the king's downfall', while the media in Bavaria, heavily influenced by the Catholic Church, painted her as 'the biggest whore in Christendom'.

Ludwig was aware of the ridiculous figure he would make in exile leaning on the arm of his young courtesan. Therefore, under extreme pressure from his ministers and the people, he issued two decrees on 17 March 1848: the first revoked Lola's rights as a Bavarian citizen and her title of Countess, while the second stated that she was to be arrested if located anywhere in his kingdom. The decrees did not save Ludwig from his pre-ordained fate, and three days later, riots broke out in both Munich and Berlin. He was forced to abdicate in favour of his son Maximillian.

Lola fled to Switzerland from where she sent letters pleading with Ludwig to join her. Though the king was broken hearted by her departure and tormented by news of her constant philandering, he decided to stay with his long suffering wife, Queen Thérèse, and their seven children.

Lola's biggest mistake was to think she could return to the fold whenever she needed to. One glance from those magical eyes and the coldest heart would melt; the enchantress would conquer all

Lola Montez photographed in California, circa 1856

before her. Now that she was settled in Switzerland, her almost hypnotic hold on Ludwig faded. He soon found a new mistress to keep the spring in his step, though he continued to send Lola 1,500 gulden every month for several years and he never demanded the return of the Wittelsach jewels he had given her (which belonged to the Bavarian people).

Lola spent the rest of her life wandering. First she returned to London where she hoped to revive her theatrical career. She set up home in the West End and secured some work in Covent Garden – playing herself in a production called *Lola Montez: an hour with the Countess*. The show ran for several months, in spite of a hammering by the critics, who called her 'La Grande Horizontal'.

Her life and career were going well until she decided to make one last bid for respectability. George Heald, a rich young man, soon to become even richer, befriended the ever-resourceful Lola. The two planned to marry, but George's family tried to spoil the arrangement by disclosing Lola's first union to a Captain James, which had never formally ended. George proved his character and married the hypnotic dancer, whereupon, she was promptly arrested for bigamy. The newspapers had a field day with this latest scandal about Lola Montez.

The newly weds fled the city, pursued by the media and the police, but the couple managed to escape to the English midlands. Unfortunately, Lola soon tired of her new husband who was a mere 21 years old, and after only a few months, their marriage was over. Poor George never recovered from disappointing her (or his family) and drank himself to death within two years.

By that time, Lola had already sailed for America and a new beginning. She was determined to restart her dancing career, and settled in New York. As only two years had passed since her expulsion from Munich, her reputation guaranteed full houses - especially when her repertoire included *Lola and the King of Bavaria*. The New York critics all agreed that she was 'not much of a dancer' yet her spider dance brought audiences into theatres for several months.

When her public grew bored with the dance routine, Lola held receptions where Americans could 'shake the hand of the Countess of Landsfeld' for as little as a dollar.

With her theatrical options becoming more limited – she was now 35 years old – she travelled west to San Francisco. Once there, she married a man she had met briefly in a New York theatre. This time, her husband was a wealthy Irish newspaper publisher named Patrick Hull. Lola said she had married him because 'he could tell a story better than anyone else I have ever met'.

Together, they moved to California, where they set up home, and for a time, Lola started cultivating a rose garden. Predictably, she became bored with domesticity, and wanted to live the high life again. She smoked Cuban cigars, ate imported foods and drank the finest liquors. She also had a pet grizzly bear (that Hull had given her) and a white parrot which she perched on her shoulders. It was the time of the Gold Rush and the ruffian miners appealed to her sensibilities - she felt like she belonged.

The extravagant couple opened a frontier saloon in Grass Valley where the interior decor included Louis XVI cabinets, Lola's pet bear, Kaneka houseboys, a large billiard table with dragons carved on its legs, and every Governor, Senator or millionaire Lola could entice into the place. The nightly show had one act - Lola at her loosest. She had developed a taste for alcohol.

Her bad temper and shocking antics did not endear her to the locals. One Grass Valley neighbour commented: "When attired in a low-necked gown as was her usual custom, even her liberal use of powder failed to conceal the fact that she stood much in need of a good application of soap."

Neither the saloon nor her marriage to Hull lasted. After a violent argument, she threw his suitcases out the window and he returned to his newspaper business. She said she was divorcing him on the grounds that 'his smell has grown less attractive than my roses'.

Lola travelled through the Sierra with her spider dance but audiences were always the same. The first performance was well attended but few came for the following shows. Her public had also grown more vulgar, and demanded that she "take it all off". In desperation, she added more tarantulas to her costume and began to remove some of the outer layers of her clothing. Her audiences continued to diminish.

When her theatrical bookings dropped off completely, she remained in the simple white cabin that Hull had bought her for almost two years. In 1958, she published her memoirs, *The Art of Beauty and Gallantry* and *Lectures of Lola Montez* with considerable success.

One of her beauty secrets for preventing wrinkles was to "tightly bind many thin strips of raw beef all about the face, covering it completely - except the eyes". The beef was to remain on the face until all the vibrant energy had soaked in. There was no mention of how long that might take.

She also embarked on a lecture tour where she said: "Let historical justice be done to the intellect of woman. I am content to leave the history of her heart and moral life, without comment, to defend itself by contrast with that of the other sex." She didn't give many lectures.

Instead, once a week, the former Countess, beloved of a king, held court in her desert cabin, gathering whoever she could into her little circle of followers. She occasionally agreed to give a performance of the legendary Spanish dances of earlier years.

Lola was almost destitute as her allowance from Ludwig had stopped and her ex-husband no longer intended to support her. She sold the grizzly bear to a circus and left Grass Valley for Australia, but this final tour was a disaster.

Australian audiences expected more from a performance than a simple dance routine. One male-only crowd booed her off the stage

*With her beauty faded and her money gone, Lola
turned to religion. This is one of the last
photographs taken of Lola Montez, 18 months
before her death in 1861.*

because she didn't remove all her clothes. In desperation, she decided that being an *artiste* meant that she could remove her clothes without losing her credibility. But nothing she did pleased her Australian audiences.

When the editor of the *Ballarat Times* made her spider dance the basis of an editorial on the lack of "public morals", Lola horse-whipped him in the street.

Before she finished her Australian tour, 'Madame Montez' was allegedly involved in the mysterious disappearance of one of her lovers from aboard a ship anchored off Fiji. Some native witnesses had seen a man being "tossed overboard" from one of the better cabins, but nothing could be clearly proven. It seems that most of the passengers had been driven off the ship by the raucous noise coming from Lola's cabin, so there was a shortage of reliable witnesses. It was time to move on.

She returned to the States and this time settled in Brooklyn, New York. She had been suffering from depression for almost a year and when her hair began to fall out, she realised she was seriously ill. Her doctor confirmed the worst, and Lola was forced to reassess her life.

She tried to make peace with her mother, who had had her stationary bordered in black since the day Lola first left India, but her mother was only interested in her sick daughter's jewels – the Bavarian diamonds that Ludwig had given her. When the gems were not forthcoming (as they had already been sold), Mrs Craigie departed for the Colonies, never bothering to contact her daughter again.

With her beauty faded and money gone, Lola turned to religion. She had exhausted all that men could offer and now it was God's turn. She joined the Episcopal Church in New York, and spent much of her time in quiet contemplation – reading the bible and visiting the outcast women in the Magdalene Asylum.

At the age of 41, she suffered a severe stroke, possibly from syphilis of the brain, which she had unknowingly contracted years earlier. In her final years, she was cared for by an Episcopalian priest who was so overcome by Lola's devotion to God, that he promised to care for her until her death. The priest was not rich however, and the famous courtesan's last years were spent in squalor of Hell's Kitchen, where her accommodation was a single room in a boarding house.

Lola Montez died on 17 January 1861, aged 42. According to the priest, her last words had been: "Tell me more about my Saviour". Her two children, who had spent most of their lives in foster care, refused to claim their mother's body.

A New York newspaper reported the death as follows:

"In a squalid boarding house in the Hell's Kitchen area of New York, Lola Montez has died. The notorious Countess of Landsfeld, once loved for her beauty and character, not her dancing, was only 42. Her lifetime had been a fable, with a little truth mixed in".

Ché Guevara Lynch
1928-1967
Guerrilla Leader with Irish Connections

Ché Guevara with Aer Lingus Hostess, Felima Archer,
who acted as an interpreter between Guevara and Irish
journalists at Dublin Airport, 19 December 1964.

When Cuba threatened to use its Soviet missiles against the United States, our planet could have been turned into a radioactive inferno, unsafe for human existence. It was the biggest crisis of the Cold War.

On Oct. 22, 1962, US President, John F. Kennedy ordered a total blockade of Cuba, threatened an invasion of the island, and placed U.S. forces around the world on nuclear alert.

One man urged Fidel Castro to use the nuclear missiles against the US and to hell with the consequences. His name was Ché Guevara Lynch, a doctor-turned-guerrilla, who, according to his father, had "Irish rebel blood in his veins".

When Washington demanded the removal of the Soviet nuclear missiles, Cuban workers and farmers responded by mobilizing in defence of their communist revolution. Behind the scenes, Kennedy negotiated with Soviet premiere Nikita Khruschev, who was persuaded to remove the missiles without consulting the Cuban government.

Ché Guevara Lynch, the communist guerrilla of Irish descent, was so disappointed that the nuclear missiles were removed from his adopted country that he never spoke to the Soviet leadership again. He also fell out with Fidel Castro, one of his closest friends, shortly afterwards.

He abandoned Cuba, and went off in search of revolution in South America, where he died at the hands of CIA-trained Bolivian soldiers more than 35 years ago and was therefore guaranteed immortality.

During his lifetime, both men and women would stop talking when the Argentinean entered a room - such was his beauty. But everyone knew he had a mad streak - that he killed 'deserters of the revolution' himself on the spot. Such was the mystique surrounding Guevara that the Bolivian authorities felt the outside world would never believe the news of his death. They ordered doctors to clean up his body, and to make it presentable for the media. But before doing so, the doctors were instructed to amputate Guevara's hands, preserving them in formaldehyde, so that his fingerprints could be verified against police records.

The haunting photographs of a Christ-like figure released to the newspapers helped to launch a legend, turning the image of Guevara into a revolutionary icon. By removing the bloodstained khaki jacket, the doctors had allowed the bullet-hole in his chest to be shown to the world's cameras. Gradually the news leaked out that Guevara had been executed after capture.

Today, the famous image of him with his long dark hair and intense gaze are as much a part of the daily scenery in Cuba as 1950s

Ché Guevara as a young doctor in 1954. He would soon depart on a tour of South America. He went to Guatemala and joined the pro-Communist regime of Jacobo Arbenz Guzmán where he earned his living working as a medical orderly and by writing articles about Inca and Maya ruins.

American cars and children in Communist pioneer uniforms. Portraits of the Argentinean hang in police stations, schools, medical clinics and government ration stores.

* * *

Argentina is the country with the largest Irish population outside of the English speaking world. Many Irish settlers arrived there before and during the Great Irish Famine. Ana Lynch, with whom Ché's family lived for years (after his father lost the family farm) and to whom Ché grew especially close, was the daughter of immigrants who had sailed to Argentina from Galway in the late 19th century. Her son, Don Ernesto Guevara Lynch (Ché's father) was born in 1900, married Celia de la Serna, and they had five children. The eldest child in the family, Ernesto Ché Guevara Lynch, was born in 1928, into an extended, but close knit, middle class family in Rosario, Argentina.

Primary school education took place at home, mostly with his mother, Celia, where he learned to speak French and basic English. He became a voracious reader of Marx, Engels and Freud, which were all available in his father's library. At secondary school, he excelled in literature and sports, particularly rugby. During these years, he was influenced by Spanish Civil War refugees and the long series of squalid political crises in Argentina which culminated in the 'Left Fascist' dictatorship of Juan Peron to whom his family were opposed.

While studying at Buenos Aires National University, the future revolutionary was touted as a possible rugby international for Argentina. His position on the University team was scrum half, and he was known as 'the little general' when he played. He received a medical degree from the University of Buenos Aires in 1953.

According to his father, he left rugby and medicine to become "a self styled general of the Americas, playing for a bigger team and for higher stakes than a rugby team."

Don Guevara Lynch put his son's revolutionary instincts down to

62

Ché with his parents, Celia de la Serna and Don Guevara Lynch. His father said he gave up medicine and rugby to fight on the world stage because he had Irish rebel blood in his veins.

63

his Irish ancestry.

"The first thing to note is that in my son's veins flowed the blood of the Irish rebels" he said in a 1969 interview.

He went on: "Ché inherited some of the features of our restless ancestors. There was something in his nature which drew him to distant wandering, dangerous adventures and new ideas". These ideas prompted him to turn his back on medicine and rugby.

Ché Guevara, aged 36, came to Dublin on 19 December 1964. At that time, he was Cuba's Minister for Industry. He, and his political entourage, were on their way from New York to Algiers when severe fog prevented a stopover at Shannon airport and their aircraft landed in Dublin instead.

Naturally, Ché's presence was given plenty of attention by the Irish media. He gave several interviews to print and broadcast journalists. During his interview with the fledgling television channel, RTE, he spoke of his Irish ancestors, the Lynches.

All the national dailies carried stories the following day. One newspaper reported: "Guevara wore a black beard of the Castro-type. The Minister, who is 36, was dressed in khaki-coloured battle dress." When reference was made to his clothes in the interview, he said defensively that he wore military style clothing "out of choice and it is not because Castro wears clothes like that."

When asked by another reporter what he would be discussing at the Tri-continental conference in Algiers, he replied "the weather".

He also refused to speak about his speech to the United Nations, given the previous day, where he advocated Marxism as the only sensible world economic strategy. Instead he spoke fondly of his wife and 5 children, and his only leisure activity, chess.

During his brief stay, he wrote a letter to his father in Argentina. It was first published in one of the books on Ché's life called *A Brave Man*.

Dear Dad,

With the anchor dropped and the boat at a standstill, I am in this green Ireland of your ancestors.

When they found out, the [Irish] television came to ask me about the Lynch genealogy, but in case they were horse thieves or something like that I didn't say much.

Happy holidays,

Ernesto.

The following year, Guevara was back in Ireland again. He arrived at Shannon Airport on Saturday, March 13th, 1965. He was with a group of 71 passengers on a Cuban Airlines Britannia aircraft which had developed mechanical trouble on its way to Havana.

When interviewed by journalists, Guevara refused to talk about politics. He wanted to go with a few friends to see the city's nightlife, and on the advice of some of the staff at the airport, he adjourned with his group to Hanratty's Hotel on Glentworth Street. According to reports, they returned 'in very good form' that evening wearing sprigs of Shamrock in their lapels. At that time, Limerick was preparing for the St Patrick's Day celebrations. Guevara and his friends flew back to Havana early the following day. He would never return to Ireland and would be dead within two years.

* * *

The CIA had already begun to keep a detailed file on Guevara - who was known to be pro-Communist - long before he had qualified as a doctor. The early passages cover his health and school activities:

"Though suffering from Asthma as a child, he underwent a programme of rigorous physical exercise under the direction of his father. These activities included mountain cycling and rugby football. Nevertheless, he still carries an oxygen inhaler with him at all times."

"Guevara participated in several revolutionary movements against the Perón regime. In his final year at medical school, Guevara and a friend called Alberto Granado, took study leave to visit leprosy and allergy clinics. It has been reported that he made the trip to escape his military obligations in Argentina."

During this trip around Latin America, he experienced first-hand, the depth of poverty and suffering of his fellows. This experience had a major influence on his political development.

"He obviously has an adventurous nature as he made the trip by motorcycle across the Andes, through Chile and Peru and by canoe along a portion of the upper Amazon to Columbia and Venezuela. His travels finally brought him to Miami, where he was turned back by US immigration authorities."

When he graduated with his medical degree, he went to Guatemala and joined the pro-Communist regime of Jacobo Arbenz Guzmán where he earned his living working as a medical orderly and by writing articles about Inca and Maya ruins.

"Guevara plainly has a strong, emotional anti-US bias and a sympathetic outlook toward Communism. He especially condemns the US role in replacing the pro-Communist Arbenz regime in Guatemala with a military junta in 1954."

The CIA file concluded:

"He fancies himself as a good judge of literature and poetry, fine foods, brandies and cigars. He frequently displays a soft-spoken manner, but despite this aura of culture, Guevara has an acute aversion to bathing and presents an unkempt and neglected appearance."

When Arbenz was overthrown in 1954, with the help of the American-CIA, Guevara was forced to flee to Mexico where he met the young Fidel Castro and other exiled Cuban revolutionaries in 1955.

In July 1956, Castro, Guevara and others were rounded up by the Mexican security police for conspiring to overthrow the Cuban government but they were released after only a few weeks. In December they embarked on the Granma expedition which sought

The earliest picture of a young Fidel Castro & Ché together in Mexico (1956) where they plotted the downfall of Cuba's Batista Regime.

In January 1959, Castro & Guevara led the triumphal entrance into Havana. The guerrilla campaign had lasted less than two years

to overthrow the Cuban dictator Fulgencio Batista.

The force consisted of just over 80 men. They sailed from Mexico to Cuba but suffered heavy losses due to attacks from Batista's army. Only 12 guerrillas landed on the island. Yet, as the rebels fought their way through the countryside, their numbers swelled. Guevara was commander of one of the largest of the five rebel columns and he gained a reputation for bravery and military prowess, second only to Fidel Castro himself. For a time, he became one of Castro's closest and trusted friends. "It will be difficult to find a man who is his equal," Castro once said of Guevara. "A revolutionary purer than he or more exemplary than he."

Guevara and his men secured the provincial town of Santa Clara in late 1958. Batista fled the country soon afterwards and the rebels knew they had won. The guerrilla campaign had lasted just over 2 years.

In January 1959, Guevara and Castro led the triumphal entrance into Havana and the Argentinean was awarded "naturalised citizenship of Cuba" so that he could serve in any new government that was formed. His first position in government was that of commander of La Cabana Fortress in Havana. There, he had jurisdiction over the notorious "war crime" trials which led to the execution of 6000 civilian and military officials. He was able to arrest, try and execute anyone "at will" under the Revolutionary Code of Justice, and he took a personal interest in the prosecutions of former members of Batista's Bureau for the Repression of Communist Activities (BRAC). He was also conspicuous in promoting political indoctrination courses along Communist lines, and is also credited with the development of Cuba's civilian militia.

As president of Cuba's national bank from 1959, Guevara was instrumental in cutting Cuba's traditional economic ties with the US and directing the flow of trade to the Communist bloc.

He then served as Cuba's Minister for Industry from 1961-65. He set up a strict licensing system to reduce imports and cut down on the outflow of dollars. He introduced measures to keep inflation low while making it impossible for the middle classes to continue to accumulate capital.

From October 1960 to February 1961, he travelled to China, Czechoslovakia and the USSR, as part of a commercial delegation to promote his ideas.

Guevara argued with Castro frequently. He was concerned that the money going into the armed forces in Cuba was not providing any financial return for the national economy, and in a television speech in 1961, he criticised Castro openly on this issue.

His intransigence towards both capitalist and communist establishments forced Castro to drop him from government in early 1965, not officially, but in practice. Guevara had grown bored with post-revolutionary life in Cuba in any case. He wanted to return to the continent, where he saw ideal conditions for a peasant revolt in both the African Congo and Bolivia, as the latter bordered five other South American countries. If he could succeed in South America or Africa, he felt he could spread unrest throughout the hemisphere. He was always happiest when promoting revolution.

He disappeared from Cuba in 1965, renouncing his Cuban citizenship, only to resurface the following year as the leader of a small band of guerrilla fighters in the Bolivian mountains.

Nobody knew of his whereabouts for almost a year. It is now known that he spent the interlude in the African-Congo trying to export revolution there. The 7-month campaign was a disaster and he moved on to Bolivia with the same purpose in mind.

From his hideout in northern Bolivia, Guevara issued what he hoped would be a stirring call to the left of the Third World "to create two, three, many Vietnams". This was at a time when the US was sending tens of thousands of its own troops to fight in Vietnam, and gradually becoming bogged down.

But he, and the few Cuban revolutionaries who accompanied him, were looked upon as "outsiders" by Bolivian nationals, and they found themselves being hunted down like common criminals. Rear-guard support from Cuba was sporadic.

He wrote to his parents: "I believe in the armed struggle as the only solution for those peoples who fight to free themselves. Many will call me an adventurer as I am one of a different sort; one of those who risks his skin to prove his platitudes." Sensing his attempt to recreate the Cuban revolution in Bolivia could be his undoing, he wrote to Fidel Castro: "Other nations of the world call for my modest efforts."

In his last letter to his children he wrote: "Grow up as good revolutionaries… always remain capable of feeling deeply whatever injustice is committed."

From March to August 1967, Guevara and his small band of guerrillas struck randomly against Bolivian Armed forces which totalled about 20,000 men. In September, the Bolivian government air-dropped leaflets offering a $4,200 reward for his capture.

The last entry in Ché's diary says that the guerrillas had run into an old woman herding goats in the Canyon of Valle Serano. They asked her if there were soldiers in the area but they were unable to get any information. Afraid that she would report them, they paid her 50 pesos to keep quiet. Ché wrote: "We have little hope that she will do so".

His last battle took place in Quebrada del Yuro. According to the legend, as Bolivian soldiers surrounded the few remaining guerrillas, Ché, who was wounded in the arms and legs, shouted: "Do not shoot! I am Ché Guevara and worth more to you alive than dead".

He and his men were taken prisoner by Bolivian soldiers who had been trained, equipped and guided by US Green Beret and CIA operatives. He was executed, along with his comrades, the following day near Vallegrande, Bolivia on October 9th, 1967.

His hands were amputated and preserved in formaldehyde so that his fingerprints could be compared with those held by the

*December 1964. The Cuban Minister for
Industry, Dr Ernesto Ché Guevara, with
his secretary, José Manrea (left) at Dublin
Airport after being diverted from Shannon
due to fog. When Irish journalists asked
him if he was imitating Fidel Castro by
wearing army fatigues, Guevara lost his
temper.*

Argentine police. The preserved hands were later smuggled out to Cuba. Today, they are displayed in Havana's Palace de Revolution where visiting dignitaries - but not the ordinary public - are allowed to view them.

That night, his body, along with those of his comrades, was buried in a mass grave beside the airstrip in Vallegrande. Bolivian officials told Guevara's family that his body had been cremated,

Later the same month, Fidel Castro delivered a eulogy in Havana to nearly a million people - one of his biggest audiences ever: "Ché's lifelong struggle against imperialism and his ideals will be the inspiration for future generations."

It was not until July 1995, that Bolivian General Mario Salinas admitted "he had been part of a nocturnal burial detail. Ché's body and those of six of his comrades were buried in a mass grave near the airstrip near Vallegrande in Central Bolivia". A subsequent article in the *New York Times* by Jon Anderson set off a two-year search to find, and identify, Guevara's remains.

In July 1997, a group of scientists and excavators found the mass grave. Ché's skeleton was easily-identified as it had no hands. The body was still partially covered by the army jacket he always wore.

Jon Anderson reported: "Before lifting the jacket, a Cuban geophysicist lowered his head in a gesture of respect. Watching journalists and local townspeople fell silent. Several scientists sobbed as the jacket was removed. Now the last chapter has been written".

Cuba marked the return of Ché's remains to Santa Clara as a state occasion, even though the government had already abandoned many of the principles he held sacred. More than 100,000 Cubans turned out for the ceremony.

In an unusually short speech, Fidel Castro praised the Argentine-born guerrilla strategist as "the paradigm of the revolutionary who is everywhere there is a just cause to defend."

Dressed in his usual fatigues, and looking sombre and grey, Castro argued in favour of Guevara's political relevance.

Guevara had an affair with KGB spy, Tamara "Tania" Bunke, who died with him in Bolivia. She was the only woman in his small band of revolutionary guerrillas and was killed in combat on August 31, 1967. Her remains, like those of the other guerrillas, were not discovered until 1997. Apparently, a post-mortem on her body revealed that she had been 4 months pregnant with Guevara's child at the time of her death. It is clear from his diaries that he never knew of Bunke's real identity.

"Ché is fighting and winning more battles than ever," he told the crowd that included Guevara's widow, Aleida March, and her children. "Thank you, Ché for your history, your life and your example. Thank you for coming to reinforce us in the difficult struggle in which we are engaged today to preserve the ideas for which you fought so hard."

At the ceremony, Guevara's daughter, Aleida said: "The guerrillas do not return vanquished. They come as heroes, always young, valiant, strong and brave."

His body is now interred in a mausoleum in Santa Clara, so that people can come to pay homage.

Naturally, Ché's status as a sexy pop icon hasn't pleased everybody. Cuban exiles in the USA see the Argentine guerrilla as a murderous interloper, responsible for the destruction of their homeland.

Jon Lee Anderson's impressive biography, *A Revolutionary Life*, shows both the passionate idealist and the cold-hearted disciplinarian who sent 55 Cuban people to their deaths, who punished errant workers with stints at a remote labour camp on the island.

The reality is that Guevara succeeded in only one revolution with the help of Fidel Castro and others. He was ruthless with deserters in war situations and shot such men himself without hesitation.

During his lifetime, he wrote several books on guerrilla tactics and socialist revolution: *Guerrilla Warfare* (1961), *Man and Socialism in Cuba* (1967), and *Reminiscences of the Cuban Revolutionary*, published after his death in 1968. His interpretation of communism changes from Russian Marxism to Chinese Maoism and then to Trotsky-ism in the space of a decade.

Even so, his *Motorbike Diaries*, telling the story of his trip around South America, have become a best seller in Cuba, Argentina and Italy. Apparently, Castro refused to allow publication of the diaries - documenting the 23-year-old's thoughts on poverty and imperialism - until 1995 because the young Ernesto displayed "bourgeois tendencies" for seducing beautiful women and cadging free meals and drinks on his travels.

Guevara's *Wartime Diaries*, written during the disastrous Congolese and Bolivian revolutions, have also surfaced in book form. So it seems, the legacy surrounding Ché Guevara will never die.

He had 5 children by his two wives. His first marriage to Peruvian, Hilda Gadea Acosta, ended in divorce. They had one child who remained with the mother. Then in June 1959, he married Cuban, Aleida March de la Torre, after they had been living together for a few years.

Apart from his two marriages, Guevara always managed to keep a mistress near him, even while on the run. His last significant relationship was his passionate affair with KGB spy, Tamara "Tania" Bunke, who died with him in Bolivia. She was the only woman in his small band of revolutionary guerrillas, and was killed in combat on August 31, 1967. Her remains, like those of the other guerrillas, were not discovered until 1997.

A post-mortem on her body revealed that she was 4 months pregnant with Guevara's child at the time of her death. It is clear from his diaries that he never knew of Bunke's real identity.

No doubt, the revolutionary with Irish ancestors, who espoused communism and despised US imperialism, would have seen the irony in that.

Dame Alice Kyteler (Kettle)
1280-1340
Mother of all Irish Witches

*Alice Kyteler married four times and could stir
men into passionate frenzies.*

In 1324, Dame Alice Kyteler from Kilkenny was
accused by Bishop Richard De Ledrede of the following
crimes: murdering three husbands, having sex with
demons, and using the skull of a beheaded robber "for
mixing her poisons and potions".

Her accomplices were caught and burnt at the stake, or
whipped through the streets of Kilkenny. But Alice, who
had many friends in high places, escaped the death penalty
and lived until old age.

During medieval times, the practice of witchcraft was an offence against the laws of God and man, but in Celtic Ireland, dealings with the unseen and the unknown had the approval of custom and antiquity.

Consequently, when the Anglo-Normans came over to the Emerald Isle, they found that the native Celts had no predisposition towards accepting the witch as an emissary of Satan or an enemy of the Church. The Irish fully believed in supernatural influences - both good and evil - and they credited their Bards and Druids with the possession of such powers beyond the ordinary.

During the Inquisition, while the Catholic Church attempted to erase all heresy and practise of the magical arts throughout its domain, no rank or class in society could be spared the appropriate persecution; the nobleman was equal to the peasant and was liable to the same punishment as the common serf - torture and death. This was especially true of the earlier stages of the Inquisition when *sorcery* rather than *witchcraft* was the crime to be punished.

A general distinction was made between the two magical arts. Sorcery was classified as an aristocratic pursuit; the sorcerer was the master of the Devil, and compelled him to do his bidding, while the witch was generally believed to belong to the lower classes. The practices of such a person lay in the shadowy borders between good and evil, and the witch was the slave of Satan, who almost always proved to be a faithless and unreliable employer.

Witchcraft and heresy were not specifically popular in Ireland until they were forbidden by the Papacy. As with most countries, when something is forbidden, it automatically becomes more attractive, and by the first half of the 14th century, a considerable portion of Ireland had become infected by a virulent wave of heresy. This manifested itself in several ways: firstly, in a denial of the cardinal doctrines of the Church with a consequent rejection of its jurisdiction, and secondly, in the heretical use of magical arts and unholy spirits.

It was about this time that Dame Alice Kyteler, the mother of all

Irish witches, began to make her mark in the Kilkenny district. The lady in question must have been far removed from the standard idea of a witch as "an old woman of outstanding ugliness"; or else her powers of attraction were very remarkable, for she succeeded in leading four husbands to the altar.

Dame Alice Kyteler was born in 1280 at Kyteler's House, Kilkenny, where her father carried on a successful banking business. Her family had come to Ireland after the Norman Conquest of 1169 and had been settled in Kilkenny City for many years. Alice's mother died young, and the child was looked after by a series of nannies. Then, when her father died in 1298, Alice, who was an only child, inherited his business and properties. She was barely 18 years old at the time.

She soon married one of her father's associates, William Outlawe, who was also a highly successful banker from Coal Market Street, Kilkenny.

Alice had chosen her first husband wisely, as he was the brother of Roger Outlawe, Chancellor of all Ireland. His position and power would later play a dramatic part in the tale of witchcraft and heresy, for which she would be charged, found guilty, and sentenced to death.

William Outlawe was twenty years older than Dame Alice when they married in 1299. He had a stepson by his previous marriage, also called William. As William Junior and Alice were about the same age, they were said to be particularly close. It was rumoured that they were lovers and that his stepmother introduced him the art of necromancy.

Shortly after her marriage, Alice decided to build an extension to their house, extending it to Kyron Street (St Kieran Street), which she developed into an public house, known to this day as Kyteler's Inn. She was a good looking, highly sophisticated woman, who knew how to entertain, and she had the female gift of manipulating men so they lavished money and jewels on her.

Kyteler's Inn soon became the meeting place for wealthy men, both young and old, who craved for the attention of the alluring Alice.

But there was a darker side to the patroness of the Inn, which was beginning to manifest itself in gossip and hearsay among the locals. They said she practised the art of Satanic rites, but this only added to her fascination and her clientele at Kyteler's Inn grew.

When William Outlawe, her husband, died suddenly under mysterious circumstances, the local people said he had forced open a cupboard in the basement of their house, and had discovered a gruesome collection of jars and bowls of evil smelling entrails.

These items allegedly included the eyes of cocks and ravens, horrible worms and sprays of deadly nightshade and dead men's hair and fragments of unbaptised babies - some of which had been cooked in a pot made from the skull of a beheaded thief. On viewing the unsavoury assortment of goods, apparently, William Outlawe had died of a heart attack.

Only a few months later, Dame Alice married another banker from Callan, Co. Kilkenny, called Adam Le Blont. By the year, 1310 Dame Alice was once again a widow as Le Blont died suddenly after a 'drinking spree'. Just as her first husband, Outlawe, had left her vast amounts of money, property and jewels, so too, did Le Bont.

Dame Alice was becoming one of the wealthiest women in Kilkenny and if gossip was to be believed, she was also the most wicked woman alive. She had gathered a brood of young maidens around her to help with the running of the Inn who active participants in Dame Alice's experiments in voodoo and necromancy.

She married her third husband in 1311. Richard De Valle was a wealthy landlord who owned extensive properties in Clonmel. The unlucky De Valle died suddenly in the prime of his life shortly after his marriage to the beguiling Alice.

The records show that he died in "an agony of convulsions" after

Petronilla of Meath was burnt at the stake in front of the Tholsel in Kilkenny on the 3rd November 1324. She was made a scapegoat for her mistress Dame Alice who had vanished.

81

attending a sumptuous banquet hosted by his wife. The day before his death, he had bequeathed all his land and properties to his beloved in his last will and testament. The local rumours appeared to be true - she could infatuate men and bring them to such a state of frenzy that they gave her all the riches they possessed.

Dame Alice was now one of the wealthiest women in Leinster. Only the Princes of the Church could command greater wealth and assets. While amassing her fortune, she had been falling deeper and deeper into the clutches of demonology. Apparently, her favourite demon was Robin, Son of Art, who was also her lover. She presided over nightly gatherings at the crossroads where living animals were cruelly dismembered and offered to demons.

The Irish sorceress married her fourth husband around the year 1320. John Le Poer was a well connected businessman in Kilkenny, who had been a regular customer over the years at Kyteler's Inn, and he, like Dame Alice's previous husbands, had fallen under her spell.

By 1323, John found himself suffering from many different afflictions. Although he was only in early middle age at the time of the marriage, he had become feeble and slow in his movements. His hair fell out in patches and what remained of his follicles had turned a silvery grey.

The children from his first marriage tried to persuade him that it was their stepmother's fault but he refused to believe their accusations at first. When his finger and toenails began to fall out, he decided his children might be right in what they said.

He went to the Friars at Saint Francis's Abbey to ask for their help. They, in turn, contacted Richard de Ledrede, Bishop of Ossory, who was a Franciscan Friar and an Englishman by birth.

By this time, Bishop de Ledrede had already held his first Synod in Ireland on the 29th of September 1320, at which he enacted several Papal Canons. One of them spoke of "a certain new and pestilential sect in our parts, differing from all the faithful in the world, filled with a devilish spirit." From this, it would seem that heresy and unorthodoxy had already made its appearance in the diocese.

His appointment coincided with the elevation of John XXII to the Papacy. Pope John believed he was surrounded by enemies who were trying to kill him by modelling images of him in wax, and thrusting pins into the models before melting them. Consequently, in several Papal Bulls, Pope John condemned sorcerers and cautioned the inquisitors against them.

He described them as people who "sacrifice themselves to demons and adore them, making images and rings from whence they draw the evil spirits by their magical art, obtaining responses from them, while demanding their help in performing their evil designs."

Bishop de Ledrede agreed with his Pope, and quickly confirmed that things were not as they should be in his diocese. While making a visitation of Kilkenny in early 1324, (to investigate the charges brought by Dame Alice's fourth husband), he discovered that "five knights and numerous nobles in the city were involved with a band of heretical sorcerers", at the head of which was Dame Alice Kyteler.

The history of the proceedings against Dame Alice and her associates can be found in a manuscript in the British Museum. The narrative is a Latin manuscript which was written during the time of the 'Kyteler Excommunication' by one of the Bishop's assistants. Consisting of forty pages of close packed print, it was published in 1843 under the title *Contemporary Narrative of the Proceeding Against Dame Alice Kyteler, Prosecuted for Sorcery in, 1324 by Richard de Ledrede, Bishop of Ossary.*

The following charges were brought against "the Dame and her infernal crew":

1. They had denied the faith of Christ absolutely for a year or a month. During all that period they believed in none of the doctrines

of the Church; they did not adore the Body of Christ, nor enter a sacred building to hear mass, nor make use of consecrated bread or holy water.

2. They offered living animals in sacrifice to demons, which they dismembered, and then distributed at a crossroads to a certain evil spirit of low rank, named the Son of Art.

3. They sought advice and responses from demons through their sorcery.

4. In their nightly meetings they blasphemously imitated the power of the Church with lighted candles, and from the sole of their feet to the crown of their heads, naming each part expressly, they concluded by extinguishing the candles and crying *Fi! Fi! Fi! Amen.*

5. In order to arouse feelings of love or hatred, or to inflict death or disease on the bodies of the faithful, they made use of powders, unctions, ointments, and candles of fat, which were compounded as follows. They took the entrails of cocks and sacrificed certain horrible worms, various unspecified herbs, dead men's nails, the hair, brains with other abominations, all of which they cooked, with various incantations, over a fire of oak-logs in a vessel made out of the skull of a decapitated thief.

6. The children of Dame Alice's four husbands accused her before the Bishop of having killed their fathers by sorcery, and of having robbed them of their senses so that they bequeathed all their wealth to her and her favourite son, William Outlawe, to the impoverishment of the other children. They also stated that her present husband, Sir John le Poer, had been reduced to such a condition by sorcery by the use of powders and unctions that he had become terribly emaciated, his nails had dropped off, and there was no hair left on his body. No doubt he would have died had a maidservant not warned him of what was happening. In consequence of this warning, he had forcibly possessed himself of his wife's keys, and had opened some chests in which be found a sackful of ghoulish and detestable artifacts which he transmitted to the bishop by the hands of two

priests.

7. The said Dame had a certain demon, an incubus, named Son of Art, or Robin son of Art, who had carnal knowledge of her, and from whom she admitted that she had received all her wealth. This incubus made its appearance under various forms, sometimes as a cat, or as a hairy black dog, or in the likeness of Æthiops, accompanied by two other men who were larger and taller than he, one of whom carried an iron rod.

According to another source, the sacrifice to evil spirits consisted of wringing the necks of nine red cocks, and plucking nine peacocks' eyes from their heads.

Dame Alice was also accused of having "swept the streets of Kilkenny before twilight", and raking all the filth towards the door of her son, William Outlawe, murmuring secretly:

"To the house of William my sonne

Hie all the wealth of Kilkennie towne."

According to the anonymous recorder of the time:

When rifling through Dame Alice's house, "there was found a wafer of sacramental bread, having the devil's name stamped thereon instead of Jesus Christ, and a pipe of ointment wherewith she greased a staffe, upon which she ambled and galloped through thicke and thin, then, and in what manner she listed"

At the end of the Bishop's inquisition, Alice Kyteler and her nefarious crew were found " by common agreement of all the judges, secular and religious, to be guilty of witchcraft and magic, of heresy and of having sacrificed to demons. For all of which she and her faction of sorcerers are excommunicated from Mother Church and their hoods are to be confiscated."

"Furthermore, Dame Alice and her disciples are condemned to be tied to the back of a horse and cart, and are to be whipped through the streets of Kilkenny, after which the chief priestess and instigator will be burned at the stake."

Alice and her coven were to be handed over to the secular

authority so that their punishment could be meted out. The Bishop made every attempt to have them arrested, but he was frustrated by their connections to very influential people.

At the time, Alice's brother-in-law, Roger Outlawe, was Chancellor of all Ireland who pulled most of the strings of political power in Ireland. Though Alice was imprisoned briefly in the dungeons of Kilkenny castle, she managed to escape and went immediately into hiding.

Bishop de Ledrede was himself arrested for making false accusations against influential citizens. He remained in Kilkenny jail for 17 days until the Lord Chief Justice of Ireland, John Darcy, travelled from Dublin to investigate the inquisition's findings. He agreed that the facts put before him contained sufficient evidence of guilt, and he declared the sentence of death over Alice Kyteler "to be just and proper". He ordered her immediate re-arrest. Dame Alice had already fled to England where she vanished without trace.

Her friends and comrades didn't have such a lucky escape. Alice's handmaiden, Pentronilla of Meath became the scapegoat for her absent mistress. De Ledrede ordered that she be burnt at the stake in front of the Tholsel in the centre of Kilkenny. Before the execution (and in the hope of getting a confession), she was flogged six times in public.

After the beatings, Petronilla confessed to the denial of her faith, and the sacrificing of her flesh to Robert, son of Art. She also admitted that she had caused certain women of her acquaintance to appear as if they had goats horns.

Though she confessed her guilt to all she was charged with, she told the Bishop that everything she had done was at Dame Alice's instigation. There was no-one in the world more skillful in the Black Arts than her mistress. Petronilla declared that William Outlawe also deserved to die as much as she did, for he was privy to their sorceries, and for a year and a day, he had worn the devil's girdle around his body.

Bishop Richard de Ledrede spent 17 days in Kilkenny Castle's dungeons, surviving on bread and water, before he was finally released in 1324.

Petronilla of Meath was burnt at the stake in the centre of Kilkenny on 3rd November 1324. Numerous other suspected persons were also pursued by the Inquisition. The anonymous narrator continues:

"With regard to the other heretics and sorcerers who belonged to the pestilential society of Robin, son of Art, some of them were publicly burnt to death; others, confessing their crimes in the presence of all the people were marked back and front with a cross after they abjured their heresy."

"Others still were solemnly whipped through the town and the market place. Others were banished from the city and diocese. Those who evaded the jurisdiction of the church were excommunicated, while others fled in fear and were never heard of after. And thus, by the authority of Holy Mother church, and by the special grace of God, that most foul brood was scattered and destroyed".

As he had been foiled in his attempts to capture and kill the high priestess of witches, de Ledrede now focussed his attention on Alice's stepson, William Outlawe. The bishop accused him of heresy, and compelled him to submit on bended knees in the streets.

By way of penance, he ordered Outlawe to hear at least three masses every day for one year, and to feed a certain number of poor people in the diocese of Ossory. He also ordered him to cover the chancel of St Canice's Cathedral with lead from the belfry to the eastward corner. Outlawe agreed to the penance, but subsequently reneged on his obligations. He was cast into prison for several years. Sir Arnold le Poer, Alice's fourth husband was next to be attacked by the Bishop. He too, was accused of heresy, and was excommunicated after a short hearing. He was committed to five years imprisonment in Dublin Castle where neither his wealth nor his influential friends could save him. He died in prison in 1331.

Alice Kyteler never returned to Kilkenny. She is believed to have died of natural causes in the Thames district of London, circa 1340.

* * *

Dame Alice was not the only Irish witch to achieve infamy. In 1327 Adam Dubh O'Toole of Leinster, was burnt alive on College Green for denying the Doctrines of the Incarnation and the Holy Trinity, and for rejecting the authority of the Holy See.

In 1353, two men were tried in Bunratty Castle, Co. Clare by Roger Cradok, Bishop of Waterford, for holding heretical opinions (and for being arrogant to the Blessed Virgin), and were sentenced to be burnt at the stake.

Queen Elizabeth's Anti-witchcraft Bill (1563) was passed in Ireland under the rule of James 1. It advocated the death penalty for murder by sorcery, and a year's imprisonment and "the pillory" for witchcraft that was not deadly. The property of an accused person was forfeit only on conviction for a second offence for witchcraft, and only in crimes of divination, attempted murder, and unlawful love. (The Bill was not repealed in Ireland until 1821.)

In 1661, the Mayor of Youghal committed an Irishwoman named Florence Newton to the town's prison after she was charged with "hexing" and torturing a young servant girl. According to the court's records, Florence boiled her own urine and poured it over the servant girl's hands to see if they would bleed. There is no record of what happened to Florence, but most likely she was sentenced to death.

In 1699, a pamphlet called *The bewitching child in Ireland*, was produced to tell the story of a 9-year-old girl who was apparently bewitched by a beggar woman. The girl went into violent fits of "vomiting all sorts of odds and ends". The beggar woman was tried, sentenced, strangled and then burned.

During 1710-11, Irish witch trials centred mainly in Island Magee, near Carrigfergus, Co. Antrim. In one trial, a devout 18-year-old girl accused eight local women of constantly "haunting" her. A Dr. Tinsdall, Vicar of Belfast gave the eyewitness account that ultimately convicted each of the eight women to a year in prison, but only after they had been flogged publicly in the streets. The story is told in *A narrative of the sufferings of a young girl called Mary Dunbar*, (1712).

The last record of witchcraft being a criminal offence in an Irish court occurred in 1911, when an indigent Dublin woman was tried and imprisoned for killing an old-age pensioner in fit of insanity.

Captain John Riley
1817-1850
Leader of the San Patricios Battalion in the Mexican-American War

The 'San Patricios' (St Patrick's) Mexican Battalion led by Captain John Riley fought under their own Irish banner 'Erin go Bragh' against the land grabbing Americans.

Captain John Riley from Clifden, Co. Galway became the self-styled leader of a band of Irish-born deserters from the US Army. They became known as Mexico's "rogue" battalion - the San Patricios. Praised for their bravery and daring in battle, most of them perished at the end of a hangman's rope.

After the Mexican-Armerican War, they were worshipped as heroes in Mexico, despised as traitors in America, and completely forgotten about back in famine-stricken Ireland.

When the first rumblings of the Mexican-American War (1846-8) began, the shiploads of Irishmen and women escaping the potato blight were streaming into America. Mexico had rejected a $15 million cash-for-land deal offered by the US and the Americans decided to strike back by annexing Texas in 1845. Mexico responded by severing diplomatic relations with its neighbour. The newly inaugurated US President, James Polk, enraged Mexico by moving 4,000 troops – half the American standing army at the time - to the Rio Grande, a river that was historically considered to be well within Mexico's borders. Thousands of Irishmen had already joined the US army at $7 a month and were marched south towards Mexico. US and Mexican troops skirmished across the Rio Grande, leading Polk to declare to Congress on May 11, 1846, that "the cup of forebearance has been exhausted. American blood has been spilled on American soil". It was a declaration of war against Mexico.

At the time, the American army was made up of volunteers, not conscripts, who had been lured by the prospect of money and the opportunity for social advancement and promotion through the ranks. Half the soldiers were recent immigrants whose patriotism must have been fragile. Almost immediately there was a high desertion rate in the lower ranks. These were filled with foreign-born soldiers - a quarter of them Irish and ten per cent Catholic Germans and Canadians. US Army officers, on the other hand, were mainly Anglo-Protestants who found the Irish foot soldiers easy targets for their prejudice and abuse. At the time, the US anti-immigrant press (heavily influenced by the English press) caricatured the Irish race with simian features, portraying them as unintelligent drunkards who were seditiously loyal to the Pope. The Irish resented the harsh treatment of Catholic priests and nuns by the ruling Protestant majority. In anti-Catholic riots in Philadelphia, about 20 people were killed and two churches burned in anti-Catholic riots in Philadelphia and a mob in Massachusetts

In 1959, the Mexican government dedicated a commemorative plaque to the San Patricios across from San Jacinto Plaza, the Mexican City suburb. It lists the names of the members of the battalion who lost their lives fighting for Mexico, either in battle or by execution. There are ceremonies there twice a year, on September 12, which is the anniversary of the executions, and on Saint Patricks Day.

pillaged and burned a convent.

The land grabbing war was an attempt by America to fulfill its Calvinist vision of "a Manifest Destiny that our nation will stretch from sea to shining sea". Catholics could not be allowed to play a big part in its determination. (Perhaps for this reason, over 150 years later, the Mexican-American war is one that the US would prefer to forget.)

Under the command of General Zachary "Old Rough and Ready" Taylor, the immigrant foot soldiers based in the south were given harsh punishments in order to maintain discipline.

Combined with intolerable, disease ridden living conditions plus General Santa Anna of Mexico's propaganda campaign - offering land, money and wives to American deserters - hundreds of Irish soldiers began to equate their cruel, Protestant officers with their former British oppressors, and chose to side with Catholic Mexico.

Just prior to America's declaration of war on Mexico, Irish Catholic soldiers stationed in Texas, routinely swam behind enemy lines, across the Rio Grande river, to attend Mass. One of these soldiers, John Riley, an immigrant from Clifden, Co. Galway decided to take up the Mexican's offer of extra pay (which went up from $7 to $57 per month) and joined the Mexican army. Riley had served in the British army in Canada, had deserted to become a labourer in Michigan, and eventually enlisted in the US army. After seven months of misery and abuse at the hands of the officers in Fort Brown, he decided he had had enough.

He was able to persuade dozens of brutalised Irish soldiers to abandon their posts and change sides, forming a Mexican foreign legion which became known as the Saint Patrick's Battalion or 'San Patricios'. As many as 300 deserters joined the San Patricios over the next two years.

At San Luis Potosi, convent nuns presented the San Patricios with a hand-stitched green silk banner. It featured "a shamork and harp, surmounted by the Mexican coat of arms, with a scroll on which was painted "Libertad para la republica Mexican". Under the harp was the motto: "Erin go Bragh". The San Patricios fought proudly for Mexico under their banner and were respected by both sides for their courage and fierce fighting ability. At the same time, they were castigated and condemned by their Irish-American counterparts for betraying their adopted nation and raising arms against their Irish brothers.

The Mexicans were able to build an effective artillery battalion around Riley and his men as both he and his compatriots had been well trained by the American Army. Riley's leadership at the Battle of Buena Vista, February 1847, was commended as "worthy of the most consummate praise because the men fought with daring and bravery". US Army General Zachary Taylor, deep in Mexico with less than 10,000 men, was surprised by Santa Anna and the San Patricios, and was forced to retreat quickly, burning most of his supplies in the process. The victory led to Riley's promotion to Captain.

The Americans counter-attacked, using modern cannister and grapeshot artillery against the inexperienced Mexican infantry. From that time onwards, the Mexican forces would be on the retreat.

Captain Riley was useful to the Mexican's, not only for his knowledge of bombardment tactics, but also for recruiting potential deserters. The Mexicans made many appeals to "American" soldiers to defect during the war. Most of the appeals were signed by President Santa Anna, but at least one was signed by John Riley himself. It was addressed: "To my friends and countrymen in the Army of the United States of America…"

"Irishmen! Listen to the words of your brothers, hear the accents of Catholic people…is religion no longer the strongest of human bonds? Can you fight side by side with those who set fire to your temples in Boston and Philadelphia? Are Catholic Irishmen to be the destroyers of Catholic temples, the murderers of Catholic priests? Come over to us; you will be received under the laws of that truly Christian hospitality and good faith which Irish guests are entitled to expect and obtain from a Catholic nation. May Mexicans and Irishmen, untied by the sacred tie of religion and benevolence, form only one people."

Riley refers to the "unholy war" and to the Irishman's "love of liberty" and to the pillaging of Catholic shrines. He implores his audience to "abandon a slavish hireling's life with a nation who, even in the moment of victory, will treat you with contumely (arrogance) and disgrace".

Throughout the war, he continued to collaborate with Mexican generals, distributing handbills urging Irish Catholic soldiers to defect from American ranks. One handbill reads:

By July 1847, the San Patricios numbered around 200 soldiers, about 60 per cent Irish-born, while the remainder were "foreign-born nationals", mainly Catholic born Germans and Canadians. The "rogue" battalion fought in five major battles, earning commendations for bravery in action and the praise of President Santa Anna who must already have known they were fighting a lost cause. John Riley was again promoted, this time to Major, the highest rank for a non-national serving in the Mexican army

Six months after the Mexican retreat at Buena Vista, American troops attempted to storm the gates of Mexico City, defended on its southern flank by the San Patricio Battalion. The Irish soldiers must have been aware of their predicament as deserters – if they were captured, they would face the death penalty. They must have decided that if they were going to die anyway, they might as well die fighting. Badly outnumbered by American troops, the Mexican army of 8,000 men began to crumble and disperse but the San Patricios stood their ground. Many were slaughtered in the battle as a result, yet, the renegades were one of the last battalions to surrender after defending a strongpoint near the convent at Churubusco for several days. More than half the San Patricios died fighting. About 85 others, including John Riley, were taken

*A major celebration was held in San Jacinto Plaza,
Mexico City in 1983, when the Mexican government
authorised a special commemorative medallion
honouring the San Patricios. The Mexican Symphony
Orchestra played the national anthems of both Mexico
and Ireland. Mexican officials eulogised the St Patrick's
Battalion martyrs, and a few words were spoken by Irish
Ambassador, Tadgh O'Sullivan.*

prisoner. A few managed to escape, but were recaptured when the Americans overran Churubusco on August 20, 1847.

Among those demanding harsh punishment, or death, were the thousands of Irish immigrants, who at that time, made up a quarter of the American Army. There were seventeen totally Irish battalions on the American side during the conflict. Many were highly decorated units such as the Emmet Guards from Albany, New York; the Jasper Greens of Savannah, Georgia; the Mobile Volunteers of Alabama, and the Pittsburgh Hibernaian Greens. They felt the Irish renegades had only served to intensify anti-Irish and anti-Catholic prejudices by their actions. Among those calling for clemency were the Archbishop of Mexico and even some US citizens resident in Mexico.

A court martial was quickly convened by order of US General Winfield Scott. He sentenced 72 San Patricios to death by hanging for treason and desertion. The decision to hang them rather than to execute them by firing squad emphasised the disdain in which the deserters were held. Many of the condemned claimed they had deserted while drunk, and for no other reason. General Scott was put under pressure to review the sentences, but there were few reprieves. Much fighting still lay ahead for the Americans and an "example" had to be set. Surprisingly, John Riley, the battalion leader was spared the death penalty. Technically, he had deserted the American Army before the war against Mexico had been officially declared.

Sixteen San Patricios were hanged on September 12, 1947 at San Angel. The next day, 30 more met the same fate. The executions were described by a foreign correspondent as "a refinement of cruelty and a fiendish prolongation of the ecstasies of revenge". The condemned men were forced to stand in mule carts, bound and gagged, with nooses around their necks for several hours. They could see Chapultepec Castle where the final battle of the American campaign was raging. The order was given that once the Stars and

General Santa Anna said that if he had more men like the
San Patricios fighting on his side, Mexico would have
won the war.

Stripes appeared over the ramparts of the Castle (replacing the Mexican flag), the mules were to be whipped, leaving the victims to swing. The flag was raised at 9.30am, and the remaining San Patricios breathed their last.

The condemned Irishmen wore their Mexican uniforms for the executions and were buried in local graves dug by Riley and a few others. Those spared from hanging were branded with the letter "D" for deserter using hot irons.(The soldier adminstering Riley's punishment 'acidentally' burned the letter into his face upside down, so he seared him a second time, on his other cheek.) They were publicly whipped and sentenced to several months hard labour before eventually being released.

The renegades who survived the war, generally disappeared from history. A handful of Irish born soldiers are on record as having taken up land claims promised to them by the Mexican government.

As for Riley, he later rejoined the Mexican Army with the rank of Major and the brevet of Lieutenant Colonel. Unfortunately, he became involved in an unsuccessful coup against the Mexican government and was discharged from the army in 1850 with back pay of 800 dollars.

Historians have assumed that he made his way to Veracruz to take a ship back to Ireland. It has also been suggested that he took up the offer of land and married a wealthy Mexican woman, and together they raised a family. But historian and author Robert Miller has uncovered what appears to be the Irishman's death certificate. Like Riley's army records, it uses the name "Juan Reley", the Spanish spelling of his name.

It reads: "In the illustrious city of Veracruz, on August 31, 1850, I, Don Ignacio of Veracruz, curate of the parish of the Assumption of Our Lady, buried in the general cemetery, the body of Juan Reley, native of Ireland, unmarried, parents unknown. He died as a consequence of drunkenness without sacrament (last rites)".

Though they fought on the losing side in the war, the San Patricios are still revered in Mexico where two annual celebrations take place to commemorate their memory. Immediately after Mexico's defeat, President Antonio Lopez Santa Anna who also commanded the armed forces, stated that if he had been able to lead a few hundred more men like the San Patricios, Mexico would have won the war.

Indeed, the Mexican-American war was one of the bloodiest battles in American history, though it serves only as a footnote in the development of that nation. Of the 104,556 "American" servicemen who fought in Mexico, 13,768 died in action – at 13%, this is the highest mortality rate ever suffered in a military campaign by the Americans.

Territorially, it was the most disastrous war in Mexican history. In defeat, Mexico lost almost half its national territory to the US – a total of 870,000 square miles. The area covers the states of California, Arizona, New Mexico and parts of Colorado and Utah. Just as devastating was the loss of Mexican national pride for a young country barely 25 years independent of Spanish imperialism.

Were the San Patricios heroes or villains? For the American Army, they were more hated than the vilest enemy soldiers and were guilty of treason.

For the Mexicans, they were, and remain, gratefully remembered heroes and martyrs who 'followed their conscience' to fight against the unjust invasion and theft of Mexican soil. Because nations and cultures only read into history what they want to take out of it, there may never be a definitive answer to the question.

Lady Mary Heath
1886-1939
World Record Breaking Athlete & Aviator

*Sophie Pierce, in her heyday - pictured
just prior to her first marriage.*

It is more than 75 years since a Limerick born woman,
Sophie Pierce - who later became known as Lady Mary
Heath - completed the first solo flight from Capetown to
London via Cairo.

She later broke the women's seaplane altitude record and
light aircraft altitude record. By that stage, she was already
a world champion highjumper and Britsh champion javelin
thrower.

Sophie Pierce also became the first female pilot to fly
for KLM Airlines. She died tragically, in a way that nobody
could have expected.

Lady Mary Heath was born as Sophie Pierce on November 10th, 1886 at Knockaderry House, near Newcastlewest, Co. Limerick. She came from an unstable background and her parents' marriage was fraught with difficulty. Her father, the son of a wealthy doctor, inherited a farm but mismanaged it until the family legacy was in ruins.

Sophie was taken as a baby to live with two of her aunts. After attending St Margaret's Hall boarding school in Dublin, she completed a degree in Agricultural Science at University College Dublin. She then began teaching at the University of Aberdeen in Scotland.

Shortly after the outbreak of World War 1, Sophie went to London to become a dispatch rider. The outfit was attached to the Royal Flying Corps and this is when she first became interested in becoming a pilot. There were no female pilots in Britain at the time.

She fell in love with army officer, William Elliot-Lynn, and married him in 1918. When the war ended, he set off to work as a manager on a coffee plantation in Kenya. Though Sophie joined him a few months later, she was unhappy with her new life in the wilderness, writing poetry to relieve her boredom, and the marriage broke down after only two years.

She returned to her job as a teacher at Aberdeen University where she helped to found the *British Women's Amateur Athletic Association* in 1922, becoming its first vice-president. Within a year, she had broken the world highjumping record (4ft 11ins) and also held the record for the British women's javelin. She had become a remarkable all-round athlete - proficient in tennis, golf, hockey and lacrosse.

She continued her promotion of women's athletics, and wrote the well-received reference book, *Athletics for Women and Girls*, which remained the standard coaching manual in British athletics for several decades. The book was based on papers she presented to the International Olympic Committee in 1925, and the preface is a lecture broadcast by the BBC on April 9, 1925.

Sophie was selected as a British representative for meetings of the International Olympic Council (IOC), and she was instrumental in the decision to allow women to compete in the Olympic Games.

"If men and women were evolved from the same parent stock, we need the same air and healthful exercises as they do," she said.

At the beginning of the 20th Century, women were traditionally banned from participating in the Olympic Games. They were forbidden from entering the playing areas or even attending the stadium as spectators.

The founder of the Modern Games, Pierre de Coubertin, declared himself against women's participation because: "if they are unable to play in every sport on equal terms with men they should not be allowed to take part at all."

This view was opposed by several International Olympic Committee (IOC) members, including the British, who supported the stand that women had the right to participate in the Games, competing in sports to suit their capabilities.

The first breakthrough in women's participation took place at the second Modern Olympics in the 1900 Paris Games, when Charlotte Cooper became the first Women's Olympic champion by winning the Gold Medal in the tennis championship. The only other sport allowed for women was golf. Although swimming was added to the programme in 1912, this symbolic gesture to women's sport continued until 1924 when the IOC decided to open its doors to a larger participation of women in the Games.

Unfortunately for Sophie, who at the time held the world high jump and British javelin records, the British Olympic Committee decided not to send a women's team to the 1924 games because of "the limited availability of events for women competitors."

In 1925, with her best years as an athlete behind her, Sophie joined the London Light Aeroplane Club. She was its first female member and made her maiden flight in August that year. She qualified for a private, or 'A' license, but the International Commission for Air Navigation had revoked women's rights to earn a commercial, or B license, in 1924.

Sophie fought the ban and the commission agreed that if she attended flight school and passed the test, she would be granted a commercial license. She succeeded in passing the test, and the commission was forced to rescind its ban on women commercial pilots in 1926. Sophie therefore became the first woman living in Britain to hold a commercial pilot's license.

Almost immediately, she set up a world altitude record for light aeroplanes at over 17,000 feet, and in the same year, was the first woman to make a parachute jump from an aircraft.

One national newspaper reported:

"Mrs Elliot Lynn [- she was still known by her married name -] landed safely in a ploughed field watched by thousands of spectators at Hereford, England.

Describing the adventure afterwards, she said:

"The sensation of landing by parachute was about the same as a jump from a six foot wall. I could have wished, however, that the ploughed field had been a little bit softer".

The newspaper commented:

"Her first attempt on the previous day almost ended in disaster. When the aeroplane had reached a height of 1,500 feet, she climbed out on to the wings, but just as she was about to jump off, the machine, developing engine trouble, began to drop rapidly. She clung on precariously and the machine skirted a hedge by a few inches and landed on a football ground where a match was in progress. Mrs Elliot Lynn only started flying in August last year".

As a professional pilot, she began to take part in flying demonstrations and races in Ireland, Britain and the Continent. *Flight* magazine reported: "It is still a common practice for women, as aviators, to be rather disdained. Mrs Elliot-Lynn has perhaps done more for her sex than any other woman".

Mary Heath pictured wearing her flying jacket, helmet and goggles with the ever present high heels in front of her biplane, circa 1925. Within a decade, she would become the first female pilot to fly with the busy passenger airline, KLM.

At about the same time, Amelia Earhart had become interested in flying in the US, and the two would compete for flying honours - though mainly on different sides of the Atlantic.

In 1927, Sophie married for a second time to Sir James Heath, a wealthy businessman. From this time onwards, she would be known in the media as Lady Mary Heath. With her husband's financial backing, she undertook a series of record breaking aviation attempts.

In November 1927, the newly married couple, set out by ship for Cape Town, South Africa with her dismantled aircraft packed in boxes.

Between February and May, 1928, aged 31 years, Lady Heath completed the first solo flight from Capetown to London via Cairo. Her epic journey was fraught with every kind of hazard. She had to fly over deserts, vast uncharted territories, with poor quality maps and the constant danger of being shot down when flying over hostile lands. She was forced for some sections of the journey, reluctantly, to accept an escort because of the very real dangers.

She had qualified as an engineer in the USA, becoming the only woman aviator with such a qualification. (Up to this time, European women were not regarded as being eligible for this aspect of the aviation business.) These engineering skills served her well on the 72-hour flight from Cape Town. During each stop on the journey, she meticulously serviced the engine of her aircraft, and on arriving in Cairo, she told reporters of her painstaking maintenance regime:

"I did the tappet clearances everyday, no matter how short the flight was and I cleaned the petrol and oil filters. Only once did I fly in the heat of the day and I never flew at less than 7,000ft to get the cool air. I ran my engine at 1,700 rpm throughout the journey and did one to three hours routine work daily".

Lady Heath was always an individual, never part of the establishment; the world at large paid little attention to her momentous flight. Although she had sent messages and telegrams

Sophie Pierce aka Lady Mary Heath - in her thirties. Alcohol problems would start to blight her life and career.

ahead of her, her flight received media attention mainly in Britain. This was partly due to the inadequacies of the postal services in Africa, which, according to Lady Heath "constituted the main dangers of the trip".

In the same year, 1928, the Irishwoman broke the women's seaplane and light aircraft altitude record, setting a new standard for Amelia Earhart, at 23,000 feet. Though Earhart had become the first woman to cross the Atlantic in 1928, she had merely co-piloted the plane. It would be four years before the American aviatrix became the first woman to cross the Atlantic, piloting the plane herself.

Earhart had first become interested in Avro Avian Airplanes in 1928 after her goodwill flight across the Atlantic Ocean to England. While there, she was in great demand by the media, but she managed to slip away quietly to meet her Irish rival, of whom she had heard so much. During their meeting, Lady Heath generously allowed Amelia Earhart to take her first solo test flight in her Avian.

The American immediately fell in love with the plane and made the Irishwoman an offer to buy it. Lady Heath, who was developing a serious drink problem and was nearly always strapped for cash, accepted Earhart's offer.

The Avro Avian was shipped back to the United States, and later that year, Earhart flew the small, open cockpit biplane across America. Today, this plane is the only flying Avian in North America. It still carries Earhart's official registration number, 7083, and Lady Heath's British registration, G-EBUG.

Shortly after her solo record breaking flight in Africa, Lady Heath went on publicity tours in England and the United States where she was received by President Calvin Coolidge. She also returned regularly to Limerick to give flying exhibitions.

Now in competition with Amelia Earhart on the world stage, she did not always receive the accolades she had once enjoyed. In fact, her rival was now overshadowing her.

Mary Heath with husband number two, Sir James Heath.

As her second marriage began to fail, the Irish aviatrix needed a salary, so she took a job as a second pilot at the fledgling *KLM Airlines* in Amsterdam. By taking this job, she became the first female commercial pilot in Europe and flew on all KLM's European commerciall routes.

"It may be merely the impatience of a woman, but is it not time we ceased to quibble about the cost of commercial flights. Today and in the future, we must have more aerodromes [airports], for without speedy communications, commercial competition is impossible," she said.

Later in the same year, without an Avro Avian of her own, she asked the British Air Ministry for a plane so she could fly solo across the Mediterranean Sea. The Ministry refused.

By 1929, when Lady Heath's second marriage had ended, she again embarked on a long tour of the USA, giving flying demonstrations and lectures. In order to raise funds to continue flying, she co-authored a book called *Woman and Flying* with Stella Wolf Murray (another pilot) but it achieved only moderate success.

By this time, the Irishwoman was known in the US as the Lady-Queen because her second husband had been a "Lord". It mattered little that they were now divorced.

The *Jacksonville Journal* reported her arrival in the town on January 4th 1929.

"Her tiny De Havilland Moth appeared as a dot in the far-off sky. Onlookers gaped from the airfield. Perfectly and mundanely, the Moth met the grass. The Queen alighted every inch the British Olympian who had flown the length of darkest Africa."

"She was clad in a colourful cretonne smock and wore high, soft leather boots. She spun the propellor while a score of men and boys stood open-mouthed in a semi-circle."

"Lady Mary Heath is tall and imposing, fresh and ruddy and brisk. She is a flyer such as the locals had never seen. She astonished

Today, this Avro Avian is the only flying Avian in North America. Lady Mary sold it to Amelia Earhart in the late 1920's when was strapped for cash. Earhart soon overtook all of Mary's flying records using this plane. It still carries Earhart's official registration number, 7083, and Lady Mary's British registration, G-EBUG.

the world one year ago by flying an Avro Avian monoplane from the Cape of Good Hope to Cairo, an amazing, puddle-jumping jaunt hard on the heels of Charles Lindbergh's solo flight across the Atlantic."

"Flying is so safe," the Lady-Queen said. "A woman can fly across Africa wearing a Parisian frock and keeping her nose powdered all the way."

The news report said that she had flown with a Bible, a shotgun, a couple of tennis racquets, six tea gowns and a fur coat in the cockpit.

"Next day," the story concluded: "in a lonely sky, the Lady-Queen and her Moth again became dots in the distance and were gone."

The flying Irishwoman was seriously injured in August 1929 in a plane crash in Cleveland, Ohio. She had entered the National Air Races in the County, during which she lost control of her aircraft and crashed through a factory roof travelling at more than 100 miles per hour. Silver plates were inserted into her skull and it was alleged that she had suffered minor brain damage. Nonetheless, she took to the air again immediately after she had recovered.

Lady Heath's third marriage was to an American aviator, G.A.R. Williams, but like her previous marriages, it didn't last. She continued to give flying exhibitions and lectures, but her star as an aviator in America was in decline, so she returned to Ireland in 1931.

Back at home, she took a financial interest in the growing Irish aviation industry and bought the newly formed Iona National Airways - originally a flying school at which she had been an instructor. The Iona venture was renamed, *Dublin Air Ferries*, but it struggled to survive due to the competitive rivalry surrounding the foundation of Ireland's national airline – *Aer Lingus*. The first Aer Lingus flight between Dublin and Britain took place on 27th May 1936.

Short of money, and dispirited after her third failed marriage,

Lady Heath returned to England in the mid-1930s to search for work. By this stage, her health had deteriorated due to a serious drink problem. She had been ill for some time when she went to live in a London nursing home in late 1938.

She died in May 1939 at St Leonard's Hospital, London, from injuries received after a fall from a London tramcar. She was 43 years of age.

Her love for Newcastle West, Limerick had stayed with her right to the end, and her last wish was that her remains were to be cremated and "taken by aeroplane from where they would be strewn over the Square" in her home town. This final wish was carried out shortly after her death.

By that time, her world records had already been forgotten, and the American, Amelia Earhart, to whom she had sold her Avro Avian, had overtaken her achievements as an aviator.

* * *

In 1979, Grainne Cronin became the first Aer Lingus woman pilot, and also the first woman captain of an Aer Lingus aircraft.

Discrimination against women in aviation has been greatly diminished, and all jobs are now open to both sexes, since Ireland joined the EU.

Agnes Clerke
1842-1907
Astrophysicist & Writer

*Agnes charmed everyone she met. She became one
of the first women to be accepted as a member of
the Royal Astrological Society.*

Agnes Clerke, a Skibbereen woman, was a brilliant astrophysicist and writer whose reputation earned her the distinction of having a crater on the moon named after her in 1881. Clerke Crater lies at the edge of the Sea of Serenity.

Her achievement is remarkable as she worked at a time when women were excluded from education in the sciences, and were refused access to the organisations in her field of study.

The task of naming features on the moon began hundreds of years ago. The father of astronomy, Nicolas Copernicus, dominates lunar geography. The brilliant Polish scientist showed us how much easier it would be for Earth to go around the Sun rather than the reverse. His theory changed everything. Today, Copernicus, the 58-mile (93-km) crater of the western plains, is one of the moon's greatest features, with rays that spread out hundreds of miles in all directions.

On the other hand, Kepler is a smaller 19-mile (30-km) crater west of Copernicus, named for the astronomer who, in the early 17th century, discovered the mathematical nature of the planets' motions. His discovery helped Isaac Newton to formulate the Law of gravity.

Albert Einstein, the originator of relativity theory, and Hubble, arguably the 20th century's greatest astronomer, also have craters named after them.

Craters are the most abundant lunar features. They have always borne human names. So far, there has only been one exception to the rule that you must be dead to have a feature named after you. The Armstrong crater is named after the Apollo astronaut, Neil Armstrong, the first human to set foot on our nearest neighbour in space.

There are also about twenty craters named after women scientists. Few of these women received the credit due to them at the time of their contributions but science has tried to make amends by honouring them on the unnamed parts of the moon.

One of the most prominent of these scientists is the 18th century German astronomer Caroline Herschel. She discovered nebulae - clouds of interstellar gas and dust, as well as eight comets. She also helped her brother, William Herschel, discover the planet Uranus. There is another crater named after the 18th century astronomer Nicole-Riene Lepaute. She predicted the exact time of a solar eclipse in 1764 as well as the return of Hailey's Comet in 1759.

There is also an Irish crater on the moon, Clerke crater, named after Agnes Clerke, a brilliant astrophysicist from Skibbereen, Co. Cork. As an astronomy writer, the Irishwoman wrote numerous articles on the 1833 Leonid meteor shower. "On the night of November 12-13th, 1833, a tempest of falling stars broke over the Earth." She also wrote several books on astrophysics which explained the planetary system in 'simple language'. For most of her professional life, Clerke was denied entry into scientific libraries and professional institutions to which she had so much to contribute.

During the 19th century, progressing to University was not an option for Irish women. For those living on mainland Britain, Girton College, Cambridge was established in 1869 but Trinity College, Dublin did not admit its first woman student until 1904.

Among professional or wealthy Irish families, it was the prevailing philosophy of the time that boys should learn mathematics, mechanics, physics, chemistry and classical languages, while girls were channeled into 'polite' subjects such as music and needlework. This arrangement allowed boys to progress to University where a range of interesting career choices (including science and engineering) were open to them. Girls, on the other hand, usually received their education at home, often under the tutelage of a governess, who would not herself have had any serious contact with scientific or technical subjects.

Although women from wealthy backgrounds could 'see' (through the activities of their male friends and relatives) how scientific life was lived - to obtain work in this area required very special determination. Firstly, a woman had to acquire the academic and technical knowledge as well as the necessary laboratory methodology, without the advantage of formal training.

Then, it was necessary to carve out a niche in a particular field, at a time when the publication of scientific books by women was unheard of. There was no easy road to success, or even any well-worn track. To achieve recognition was a pioneering activity without any obvious ground rules. This makes Agnes Clerke's achievements in astrophysics all the more remarkable. Her brilliant works, including the book, *A Popular History of Astronomy during the Nineteenth Century*, remain unsurpassed in the field of astronomy.

* * *

Agnes Mary Clerke was born on 10 February 1842 in Skibbereen, Co. Cork, the youngest daughter of John William Clerke (a classics graduate from Trinity College Dublin) and his wife Catherine Deasy, a gifted Irish musician. The three children of this cultured family, Aubrey St John, Ellen and Agnes, responded in individual ways to the highly intellectual atmosphere of the household where they received a private education.

The Clerke children had many material advantages over others. The house in Skibbereen contained a large library containing the classics in literature and science, with technical equipment (microscopes and telescopes) and encyclopedic collections from the world of nature.

No doubt, Agnes became initially drawn to the subject of astronomy through the influence of her father who mounted a four-inch telescope in the family garden. The Clerke children could view such wonders as Saturn's Rings and the Satellites of Jupiter. They spent their early lives in 'an environment of scientific suggestion'. The inclination in the direction of science encouraged by their father was balanced by the influence of music exerted by their mother Catherine. She was acclaimed for her rendition of old Irish airs on the harp and piano and was responsible for giving her children a lifelong love of music – Agnes became proficient in piano playing, and her sister, Ellen played the guitar.

By the time she was fifteen years old, she had already written the first few chapters of the *History of Astronomy*. Her desire to examine 'science in general' was stimulated by her perusal of Joyce's *Scientific Dialogues*, while in the field of astronomy, Sir John

Almost every crater on the moon is named after a famous person, though not all of them are named after astrophysicists or dead people. Neil Armstrong, the first man to walk on the moon, 1969, has a crater named after him, as does Buzz Aldren, the second man on the moon. Clerke crater, named after Skibbereen woman, Agnes Clerke, lies next to the Sea of Tranquility

121

Herschel's *Outlines* provided her earliest reference book.

In 1861, the Clerke family moved from Skibbereen to Dublin, then in 1863, they moved to Queenstown (Cobh) in southern Ireland. Due to her delicate health, Agnes, with her mother and sister, spent at least six months of each year from 1867 to 1877 in Italy. The winters of 1867 and 1868 were spent in Rome, those of 1871 and 1872 in Naples; the next four winters in Florence; and the summers of 1874-6 at the Bagni di Lucca. In Italy, the sisters devoted themselves to literature, languages and music. During her time on the Continent, Agnes became fluent in several European languages including Italian and Latin, Greek, French and German.

In 1877, the Clerke family settled in London at 68 Radcliffe Square, and it was there - in the intellectual atmosphere that pervaded the household - that Agnes Clerke's prodigious talents thrived. In April 1877, she wrote an article called 'Brigandage in Sicily' (a work on the Sicilian Mafia) which was accepted for publication by the prestigious *Edinburgh Review*. This was followed in the same year by an article on 'Copernicus in Italy'. Her writing was highly regarded and she became a regular contributor to the journal. Over the years, she provided more than fifty articles, including many devoted to science and astronomy.

As her interests were wide ranging, she wrote on topics as diverse as 'The Origin and Wandering of the Gypsies', 'The Future of the Congo', 'Earthquakes and the New Seismology' and 'Scandinavian Antiquities'. The thirst for knowledge she displayed in researching so many subjects had its roots in her early childhood experiences. She explained in a letter to a friend:

"In the scientific sense, I had no education, but just picked up what came my way. I had a childish passion for natural knowledge and read the books accessible to me in my father's library, taught myself some elementary mathematics, and that was all. I was also very delicate growing up and never went to school, but I had private instruction in languages and music. In Italy, I undertook some serious work and contributed on various topics to the *Edinburgh Review* from 1877. An article on the 'Chemistry of the Stars' made a turning point. The studies for it revived my astronomical tendencies. Messrs. Black accepted my proposal to write a history of recent astronomy for them, and so I went on."

'The Chemistry of the Stars', which appeared in the *Edinburgh Review* in October 1880, contained the germ of her first important book *A Popular History of Astronomy during the Nineteenth Century*. The aim of this work published in 1885, was to provide an account of the development of astronomy since the time of William Herschel – starting with his research into the structure of the Universe, advancing on to spectroscopic discoveries relating to the nature of stars and nebulae.

Though 18th century astronomical knowledge had evolved by the aid of Calculus, Clerke considered this to be "too remote from ordinary experience" to support popular treatment. Although she respected this body of knowledge and described it as "having a fundamental importance that can never be diminished and should never be ignored", she felt it was not popularly accessible. This branch of the subject could be readily described to the public in simple language and her concept was to write a 'popular' (non-technical, non-mathematical) book that would provide a service to astronomy and engage the general reader.

"To help one single mind towards a further understanding of what has fascinated all ages might be an object of noble ambition" she wrote. Since she was fluent in almost every European language, she was able to quote (and translate) from primary sources which gave her book a seal of authority.

Her first book was described by scientific (male) writers as a 'masterpiece' bringing her to the attention of the professional astronomical community in Britain. That the successful author of such a remarkable text was professionally completely unknown and had never made spectroscopic observations herself caused a sensation.

Sir David Gill, one of the leading astronomers of the day, invited Clerke to spend time at the Royal Observatory in South Africa so she could learn the art of night observing and to make spectroscopic observations. He did this in spite of his long held belief that "no woman could do justice to this noble science".

In a letter to a friend, he wrote:

"She plays the piano most exquisitely as well as being one of the ablest women and most original thinkers that I ever met."

Gill was sufficiently impressed by Clerke to suggest to his professional friends in England that "a case might be argued, based on her book, to entitle her to the award of a medal by the Royal Astronomical Society". In 1888, there was extreme delicacy in suggesting such an honour for a woman and the idea was immediately rejected. (Fifteen years would pass before the idea could finally be considered.) In the interim, lobbying on behalf of women resulted in a grudging concession to issue cards of admission for meetings "to such persons as it may be thought desirable to admit".

In 1890, Agnes Clerke and Margaret Huggins (1848-1915), also an Irish astrophysicist, became founder members of the *British Astronomical Association* which provided the kind of facilities and organised events - without any discrimination of gender - that allowed anyone interested in astronomy to pursue and advance in the field. It also provided a library so women from all classes could have access to scientific books.

Meanwhile Clerke went on to write book after book. *The System of the Stars* (1890) dealt with the content and structure of the visible Universe. The moral tone of the text, which reflected deep religious convictions, indicated that even though she was a scientist, she believed in God as the creator of the universe. This book was less well received than her first, yet, two years after its publication, the Royal Institution awarded Clerke the *Actonian Prize* (one

Agnes Clerke, wrote numerous articles on the
1833 Leonid meteor shower: "On the night of
November 12-13, 1833, a tempest of falling stars
broke over the Earth."

hundred guineas) for her written contributions to the field of Astronomy. Apparently, no one who met her could resist her enthusiasm, and she began to enjoy the personal friendship of many important astronomers who were 'beguiled into acting as her editors rather than her critics.'

Her output as a writer continued to be prolific. *Familiar Studies in Homer* in 1892 (containing translations by the author from the original Greek) was followed in 1895 by a biographical work with an astronomical background – *The Herschels and Modern Astronomy*.

Problems in Astrophysics, which appeared in 1903, sought to bring the progress in astrophysics up to date. In this book, Clerke rebuked professional astronomers for their 'neglect of certain important questions'.

"The globe is studded with observatories, variously and admirably equipped, yet, innumerable objects in the sidereal heavens remain neglected."

That she was now setting the agenda for professional astronomers, while bringing them up to date on the basic background to their science, showed how far she had come from being patronised by the same community some fifteen years earlier. Rather than being criticised for her temerity, she was finally invited to become an honorary member of the Royal Astronomical Society.

Sir David Gill wrote:

"I do not believe that there is a man living who knew beforehand all the facts that you have brought together, and brought together so well in their proper places".

Honorary Membership of the Society, which was also conferred on Margaret Huggins, represented a considerable breakthrough for women scientists.

"Both these high achievers were already in the category of 'card carrying' persons with the right to attend meetings as mute spectators, when their achievements (which could no longer be ignored), caused them to be promoted from this curious grey area to the prestige of honorary membership."

In 1905, a revised edition of Clerke's *The System of the Stars* was published, as well as a new work called *Modern Cosmogonies* – an historical account of theories of the evolution of the universe, written in a philosophical and spiritual tone. At about the same time, on the basis of earlier contributions to the *Encyclopaedia Britannica* (for which she had written scholarly essays on famous scientists), the Irishwoman was chosen to contribute the main article on the 'History of Astronomy' for the eleventh edition. She was also asked by the editors to write thirty biographies of great astronomers.

The compilers of *The Dictionary of National Biography* (begun in 1882) also used her as a trusted contributor, and overall, she provided 165 astronomical biographies to the annual. During the same period, she made regular contributions to *The Observatory Magazine* while articles for non-scientific magazines also added to the prodigious output from her pen.

Clerke's final book, *The Annual Index of Astronomical Literature*, was published in 1905. Containing over two thousand references, it was collated using more than three hundred separate publications. She commented during the writing: "year by year, details accumulate, and the strain of keeping them under mental command becomes heavier". She had fallen seriously ill, which meant she could only work on the text for half-hour periods. Then, a neglected cold gradually led to pneumonia with associated complications.

Agnes Clerke died on 10 January 1907 before the publication of the eleventh edition of *Encyclopaedia Britannica*, to which she had contributed so much. Her last Will and Testament (written on 21 March 1906) provided a revealing insight into a very private part of her life – that is, her long devotion and financial support for the Catholic Church .

Given her exclusion for so many years from the Royal Astronomical Society, Clerke's obituary in the *London Times*, dated 22 February 1907 is noteworthy:

"She will be missed at the meetings of the Royal Astronomical Society, at which she was a constant visitor, where her clear judgement was at times called on to determine the value of some new suggestion in the domain of celestial physics. No other writer could have done the work of collation and interpretation of this enormous mass of new material. She pointed the way to new fields of investigation, often by one of her suggestions sweeping aside a whole sheaf of tentative conjectures".

As recently as 1984, historian, B Osterbrock, described Agnes Clerke as "the chief astronomical writer of the English speaking world". The quality of her writing, based on its extraordinary level of background reading in many languages, allowed her to surpass her original main objective – to describe modern astronomy to the public in 'simple language'.

Irish Slaves
during the reigns of
Elizabeth 1 & Cromwell

*A British Colony Slave Ship during the reign of
Oliver Cromwell. It was on such vessels that
Irish people were transported from Galway Bay
to the Sugar Islands*

During the Elizabethan and Cromwellian eras, an estimated 50-80,000 Irishmen and women died as slaves on the British island colonies known today as the West Indies. On St Kitt's Island alone, an estimated 25,000 Irish died due to exhaustion from overwork, disease, or from wounds inflicted by their British masters.

A monument has recently been built on the island to commemorate the souls of the dead. Today, the descendants of early Irish slaves, known as 'Redshanks', still form the poorest stratum of society in Barbados and other parts of the West Indies.

Dear Reader,

After the Battle of Drogheda in 1646, the British slave ship Abraham sailed from Galway Bay in the fading twilight, leaving behind the families who would never see their loved ones again.

As many Protestants were slaughtered in the battle, the large vessel was crammed to capacity with we, the unfortunate Irishmen and women who had been branded "rogues, rebels and enemies of all Protestants" by the Defender of the Faith, Oliver Cromwell.

From the bow of the ship, we saw the Twelve Pins for the last time, as the ship sailed southwards towards the Great Atlantic Ocean.

Girls and boys as young as twelve years of age, plucked from their parent's arms, made up a quarter of our passengers.

In fear and desperation, a few men jumped overboard in an attempt to swim back to land, but this was an act of folly, after several days at sea. We thought the British would shoot them for attempting to escape, but then the Captain yelled: "Don't waste your gun powder. Let them drown!"

Without blankets, or much food to speak of, our bodies clung together for warmth, and God must surely have been with us, as it did not rain for almost a week on the endless journey to the New World. We heard that it is known as the British Colony of the Sugar Islands.

The nights were shivering cold as we lay like dried fish in a bucket, pressed closely together to ease the deep chill in our bones.

Each day, we looked toward the hold where luxuries of preserved fruit and meats were kept for the officers and the merchants. We survived on leftovers - a few dried biscuits and some stale bread with dripping.

It did not help our spirits when we looked toward the stern of the vessel, where the armed mariners stood in a line, pointing their heavy muskets in our direction, lest we make any sudden movements.

We heard that the British merchants who carried us received £3-5 for each of our heads, and that once we reached our destination, we *would be resold upon the open market to men known as "British Planters."*

After several weeks of pure misery, with barely enough food to stay alive, the cold days and nights turned suddenly to endless hot days under the scorching sun. Soon afterwards, we set to land on the island named "Barbados".

Many of us were sold in bulk to the largest plantation owner, a Lord Bartholomew, though we soon learnt from our masters, that "his Lordship" is rarely in residence.

After only a few hours rest, both men and women were put to work on the deforestation of the land. The hot sun made it heavy work, and after only a few days of it, none of us believed that we would make it to the end of our seven years of bondage.

The work is slavery, pure and simple, though as baptised Catholics, we Irish cannot be called "slaves" because the Christian Churches forbid it.

Only our poor, heathen, cousins from Africa, who remain in bondage until they die, can be given that invidious title. We are known as "bonded servants" though it amounts to the same thing.

Our masters decide how much food we eat each day, when, if at all, we can receive medical attention, and what type of corporal punishment we receive. The clever Irish keep their mouths shut and work until they are ready to drop, lest they get a lash of the whip – or worse.

Many have died from exhaustion, malnutrition, dehydration and wounds which never healed since the day of their infliction. Bodies are buried quickly in large ditches before they start to smell in the unforgiving heat. There is no time for words of prayer before the dirt is thrown over them.

Our Negro cousins receive better treatment than we do as they are "slaves for life" and therefore must be handled with care. The masters work us Gaels until we are half-dead because we may only be kept in bondage for a certain period until they give us back our liberty.

They want to be sure they get their money's worth.

If a woman or girl is lucky, she is sent to work as a domestic servant in the house of her master, but there she is forced to "give favours" to both the master and his merchant friends.

Some of the women say this is preferable to the long hours on the plantations where there is little food or sustenance of any kind. Also, the beatings are usually less frequent and less severe.

Some of the better-looking Irish girls are used as harlots for the managers of the smaller plantations. Others have been used to breed with our African cousins so that the British Colony has more "slaves for life" to carry on its destiny.

If we Gaels are lucky enough to gain knowledge of the female gender, it is forced upon us, and not of our own choosing. Personal 'relations' are allowed only for the purposes of producing "more servants for the British Crown". At all other times, we are separated from our opposites. It is a truly miserable existence.

We Irish are known as "red legs" or "red shanks" because our fair skin is prone to blister under the unforbidding sun, and our back breaking work in the plantations leaves our knees swollen and bloody at the end of each day's work.

The servants who try to escape are branded with the letters "FT" for Fugitive Traitor on their foreheads. Some have been strung up by their hands while their feet are set on fire. It matters not that their feet cannot function afterwards, as only the hands are required for planting and harvesting of the vegetable crops. It also matters not if an Irishman has to crawl on his knees, so long as he does it quickly.

One hundred Irish slaves caught practicing Catholicism, have been sent to the uninhabitable Crabs Island to die of starvation. They will not be seen again.

Though the British Planters call Barbados the true paradise mentioned in the bible – because of the vast sums of money they make from their sugar crops - for us Gaels, it is truly a hell on earth. We know that we will never return to the land of our birth.

Under Elizabeth 1, the English increased their Irish "labour market" through a series of laws which enforced the conscription of "tinkers, jugglers, peddlers, wanderers, idle labourers, beggars, and such as could not give a good account of themselves".

133

The leader of the Negros has asked us to join him in a rebellion to gain freedom from our mutual oppressors. Several of us Irish have agreed. Though we have little weaponry, and the plan seems to be impossible before we begin, we are united in our efforts to win back our liberty.

I have written this testament in the event that I may not return.

May God have mercy on our souls!

***

Between the reign of Elizabeth 1 of England and the restoration of the monarchy in 1660, an estimated 50-80,000 Irish men, women and children were shipped to Barbados as slaves of the British Empire. Since the foundation of the colony in 1627, obtaining the labour required to clear the rain forests for planting crops such as indigo, tobacco, sugar and cotton, had posed a serious problem

The Christian idea at the time was that only non-Christians could be slaves, and as most of the Irish were baptised Catholics, they were technically known as "indentured servants".

Under Elizabeth, the British increased their "labour market" in Ireland through a series of laws which enforced the conscription of "tinkers, jugglers, peddlers, wanderers, idle labourers, beggars, and such as could not give a good account of themselves".

In January 1637, Irish servants on the ship *Abraham* were sold on the open market at Destination's End for £7 per head. But during Oliver Cromwell's heyday, the Irish could be sold to merchant captains for as little as £3-5 each, plus feeding for the voyage.

After the Battle of Drogheda, 1646, when many Protestants were slaughtered by Irish rebels, Cromwell increased the numbers of Irish under conscription to include "all enemies of the Crown, Roman Catholic priests, peasants whose farms had been procured for plantations, political rebels and the unemployed or dissolute from the towns."

In his own words, he had put down the Drogheda rebellion with cruelty and savagery: "the officers were knocked on the head, every tenth man of the soldiers killed, and the rest shipped to Barbados".

According to British state papers: "it was a measure beneficial to Ireland, which was thus relieved of a population that might trouble the planters, and of great benefit to the sugar planters, who desired the men and boys for their bondsmen, and women and girls in a country where they had only Maroon women and Negresses to solace them".

During the 1650s, the Governor of Galway, Peter Stubber, employed men "to take people out of their beds at night to sell them for slaves to the Indies". In 1656, when Cromwell was asked by British Planters to send 1,000 "Irish wenches" to Barbados, the Protector of the Protestant Faith replied confidently that "1,500 boys aged twelve to fourteen could also be captured and sent."

The victims of Cromwellian deportation ranged from political and military prisoners to anyone who might burden the public purse: orphans, widows and the unemployed.

From 1648 to 1655, over 12,000 Irish 'political' prisoners were shipped to Barbados. From there, they could be distributed among the other British-owned islands. These prisoners made up for a serious labour shortage caused by the English planter's lack of access to African slaves. The Dutch and Portuguese had dominated this trade in the early 17th century and most white landowners in Barbados and the neighbouring islands were unable to purchase slaves of African origin.

Numbers vary, but reliable estimates put the number of Irish shipped out to the Sugar Colonies at between 30,000 and 80,000 persons. In 1641, Ireland's population was 1,466,000. By 1652, it was down to just 616,000. The sword, famine, hardship and forced deportation had all taken their toll.

Indentured servants were known as "stock" and were matched with other servants for forced breeding. The British Planters preferred Irish labour at the time because it was cheaper than African labour, though from the 1650s onwards, the African trade took over.

Though numerous English and Scottish subjects were also deported, the harsh and often vindictive treatment of Irish deportees left a bitter historical residue. Masters in the Sugar Islands could sell and trade their Irish servants, gamble them away, flog them occasionally to death, and "generally demonstrate the complete ownership of their bodies."

The usual length of enforced bondage lasted seven years, though owners of servants could easily exploit the legal system to extend the indenture indefinitely. It was not until the *Act for Obtaining the Rights between Masters and Servants (1661)* that the dead bodies of indentured servants could be investigated with a view towards assessing the master's culpability.

Once Irish servants were freed from slavery, they rarely returned to Ireland because few could afford the passage fare home.

By the third quarter of the 17th century, the British had begun to view Irish slaves as "very seditious and prone to starting rebellions". In the Leeward Islands (Antigua, St Kitts and Nevis) there was an upsurge in friction between the Protestant English and Catholic Irish especially as England's enemies (France and Spain) were also Catholic. Anti-Irish attitudes resulted from a fear of insurrection, especially after the successful revolts of Irish servants on St Kitts in 1666 and on Montserrat in 1667. As a result, the British passed a series of laws preventing the Irish from progressing once they had been liberated from their 'bondage'. In 1701, legislation adopted on Nevis prevented 'papists' and reputed papists from holding public office or coming to the island as settlers.

The British Crown abolished slavery on 1st August 1834, but before it did so, tens of thousands of Irish people died on Barbados, St. Kitts and Jamaica. They perished in the tropical heat, from disease and overwork and from torture at the hands of their masters.

*In 1646, Cromwell increased the numbers of
Irish under bondage and enforced
emigration to include "all enemies of the
Crown, Roman Catholic priests, peasants
whose farms had been procured for
plantations, political rebels and the
unemployed or dissolute from the towns."*

Today, Irish surnames and placenames remain common throughout the West Indies – Kelly, Hogan, Flanagan, Sweeney and Cork Hill, Dublin Road, Athenry Ridge, Leitrim Road etc – yet, it would be difficult to estimate the number of Irish descendants now living in the former Colonies after more than three centuries of integration.

At the height of its powers, the British used Montserrat as a dumping ground for the 'rebellious Irish' who refused to conform to the Protestant faith. So, to a unique extent, Irishmen ruled the island of Montserrat. During the 17th century, at least six of its governors were born in Ireland. In 1673, Governor William Stapleton, originally from Thurlesbegg, County Tipperary, commissioned a census which estimated that 1,900 Irish people were living there at the time. The area around Kinsale contained the heart of the community with 88%, while St Patrick's and the hills above it were, on average, 66% Irish.

For the servants who laboured on the southern estates, Kinsale served as a provincial capital where small shops and 'tippling houses' catered to Gaelic tastes. Further south, the lands known as O'Garro's and Roche's estates were 98% Irish. This inhospitable area is where many 'free' men and women settled at the end of their servitude, living in thatched, wattle-and-daub cottages - they grew food and cash crops on small plots of dry, hilly ground.

Because they could enjoy freedoms unavailable to them on the other islands, some prosperous Hibernians became Planters and African slave owners themselves. But the vast majority of the Irish on Montserrat never became planters. Most were indentured servants, often bound to fellow-Irishmen for their contracted term. In 1678 - of the 2,682 whites living there, 1,644 were bonded or indentured.

Up until recently, the island celebrated two events on St Patrick's Day: the first was a traditional festival commemorating Ireland's patron saint; the second was a re-enactment of a failed rebellion by black slaves against their Irish masters. The fight for freedom, which began on 17th March 1768, was quickly crushed because the plan had leaked out before it could get underway. Nine African slaves were executed immediately after the aborted revolt. (In 1995, the volcano on Montserrat erupted and two-thirds of its inhabitants were permanently evacuated so these celebrations no longer take place.)

By the early 18th century, many of the Irish poor had drifted off to South America seeking their fortunes, though a significant number remained to farm the hilly backcountry - gradually intermarrying with their Black neighbours. Over the centuries, their descendants known as the 'Black Irish' have become genetically absorbed into the African population, leaving only their names as reminders of a once flourishing Irish community.

Heroes & Villains

Index

A

B

Belfast
    Dr. Tinsdall, Vicar of 90
Bishop Richard De Ledrede 77
Blanche Hillyard 28
Bolivia
    Quebrada del Yuro 70
Bunratty Castle 89

C

Captain John Riley 91
    Chapultepec Castle 98
    "D" for deserter 100
    Erin go Bragh 94
    guilty of treason 101
    hanged at San Angel 98
    Mexican-American War 91
    President Santa Anna 95
    publicly whipped 100
    Saint Patrick's Battalion/ San Patricios 94
Charles Goodyear 27
Ché Guevara Lynch 59
    Argentina 62
    as a young doctor 61
    asthma as a child 65
    Dublin Airport 71
    Bolivian mountains 69
    Buenos Aires National University 62
    Celia de la Serna 63
    CIA-trained Bolivian soldiers 60
    Fidel Castro 59
        Cold War. 59
    John F. Kennedy 59
    Limerick 65
    Marx, Engels and Freud 62
    Minister for Industry 68
    Motorbike Diaries 74

M

About the Author

Siobhán Mulcahy MA, lectures in Politics and Journalism in the Media Department at *Dún Laoghaire College of Further Education*. Her feature articles have appeared in most of the national newspapers in Ireland.

Some of her stories in this book have previously appeared in edited version, in *Ireland on Sunday* newspaper: 'Jack the Ripper was Irish'; 'Mary Heath, Record Breaking Aviatrix'; 'Lena Rice, Forgotten Wimbledon Champion' and 'Irish Slaves under Cromwell'. The Mary Heath story has also been published in *Southside People* and the book, *The Silver Lining*, edited by John Haughton.